S0-BNW-203

DARK SOLILOQUY

The Selected Poems of Gertrud Kolmar

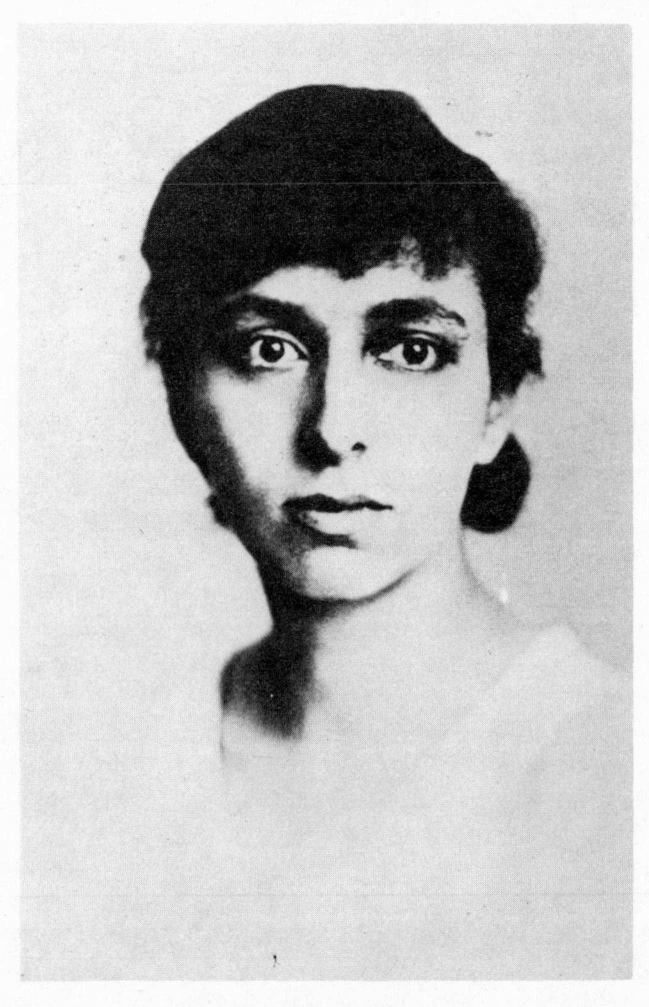

Gertrud Kolmar, 1894–1943

DARK SOLILOQUY

The Selected Poems of Gertrud Kolmar

Translated and with an Introduction by

Henry A. Smith

FOREWORD BY CYNTHIA OZICK

A CONTINUUM BOOK

The Seabury Press / New York

The Seabury Press
815 Second Avenue
New York, N. Y. 10017

Editor: Michael Roloff
Designed by Paula Wiener

Grateful acknowledgment is made to *Ms.* and other magazines where translations of some of these poems have appeared.

Library of Congress Cataloging in Publication Data

Chodziesner, Gertrud, 1894–
  Dark soliloquy.

  (A Continuum book)
  English and German.
  Translation of Das lyrische Werk.
  Bibliography: p. 261
  I. Smith, Henry A. II. Title.
PT2605.H54A27   831'.9'12   75–2239
ISBN 0–8164–9199–2

Contents

ROSE SONNETS/BILD DER ROSE

PRUSSIAN COATS OF ARMS/PREUSSISCHE WAPPEN

WORLDS/WELTEN

Foreword

> Thus saith the Lord God: Come from the four winds, O breath, and breathe upon these slain, that they may live . . . and the breath came into them, and they lived, and stood up upon their feet, an exceeding great army. Then he said: . . . these bones are the whole house of Israel . . . Behold, O my people, I will open your graves, and cause you to come up out of your graves . . . into the house of Israel.
>
> —Ezekiel, Ch. XXXVII, 9–12

A dream of reversal, of reconstruction: who has not, in the thirty years since the European devastation, swum off into this dream? As if the reel of history—and who does not see history as tragic cinema?—could be run backward: these mounds of ash, shoes, teeth, bones, all lifted up, healed, flown speck after speck toward connection, toward flowering, grain on grain, bone on bone, every skull blooming into the quickness of a human face, every twisted shoe renewed on a vivid foot, every dry bone given again to greening life. Ezekiel's vision in the valley of bones.

An imagining with the immensity of "an exceeding great army." Who rises up, what? Populations; a people; a civilization. And everything unmade, undone, unwritten, unread. The children did not live to do their sums, the carpenters did not live to cut the doors to fit the houses that the architects and engineers left in midair, in midmind. Unwritten alphabets clog the breath of this dream like so many black hosts of random grit—letters still inchoate, not yet armied into poems, novels, philosophies. Torrents of black letters fill the sky of this imagining like a lost smoke. And singular voices, lost.

Every now and then, though, the dream becomes enfleshed: a voice comes up out of its grave, the living mind resumes its dialogue with history. Anne Frank, most famously; Emmanuel Ringelblum's Warsaw Ghetto diaries; Yitzhak Rudashevski's Vilna Ghetto diaries, begun at the age of fifteen. But these recovered voices yield direct records of the harrowings. Ezekiel's vision wonders something else: how would the historian Ringelblum have written that history had that history not riven him? What would the mature Anne Frank's novels—she *would* have become a novelist—turn out to be?

The marvelous recovery of Gertrud Kolmar's poetry signifies the redemption of just such a ripened art.

Gertrud Kolmar died in Auschwitz at age 48; she was given time to become herself, though no time for her name to grow; until this moment, she must be considered unknown. She was published and reviewed barely eight weeks before *Kristallnacht,* that infamous country-wide pogrom called the Night of the Breaking Glass—after which her external precincts narrowed and narrowed toward death. Not so the open cage of her spirit: she felt herself "free in the midst of . . . subjugation." A forced laborer in a Berlin factory, she continued to make poetry and fiction. Ghettoized in a tenement, she began to study Hebrew, and her last—lost—poems were written, most remarkably, defiantly, and symbolically, in the language of the house of Israel.

What has been recovered is not the record of the harrowings—though there is this besides—but the whole blazing body of her poetry, unconsumed. The American poet she is most likely to remind us of is Emily Dickinson —and not so much for her stoic singleness, the heroism of a loneliness teeming with phantasmagorical seeing, but for the daring pressure she puts on language in order to force a crack in the side of the planet, letting out strange figures and fires: she is a mythologist. To fathom this, one must turn finally to the Blake of the *Four Zoas,* or perhaps merely to German folklore: Kolmar too invents fables and their terrible new creatures, intent on tearing out of the earth of the Dark Continent of Europe its controlling demons.

How the devils cry, oh how the deserts cry!

On and on the furnaces of destruction burn; nothing can make them go out, as long as there are you and I to remember who lit them, and why. But now and then a congeries of letters plunges up out of the sparks to give us back a child; a man who meditates on Spinoza in the slave-factory (it was to him Gertrud Kolmar talked of freedom in subjugation); a woman who fabricated original powers in a life beaten out of isolation, sans event until the last cataclysm—and who flies up alive from the cataclysm on the sinewy flanks of these poems.

As if the ash were to speak:

Amazed, I clothe myself.

CYNTHIA OZICK

Acknowledgments

For much of the biographical data to follow I am indebted to Gertrud Kolmar's sister, Hilde Wenzel, and her epilogue to *Das lyrische Werk* (1960), as well as to Johanna Zeitler and her commentary to *Briefe an die Schwester Hilde.*

Gertrud Kolmar's Life and Works

> I seek, probably with insufficient strength,
> to create for eternity.
>
> Gertrud Kolmar in a letter
> of July 23, 1941

GERTRUD, the first child of Ludwig and Elise Chodziesner, was born in Berlin on the tenth of December 1894. Her father was a successful criminal lawyer in the imperial capital around the turn of the century. The Chodziesners were a family of petty tradesmen from the Prussian provinces east of the Oder, and must once have lived in the Polish town of Chodzież, or Kolmar, as it was called under German rule. Gertrud's mother, born Elise Schönflies, descended from a prosperous mercantile–intellectual family that was long settled in the province of Brandenburg.

The young girl, who would write under the name Gertrud Kolmar, grew up in comfortable bourgeois surroundings on the affluent west side of Berlin. Although afforded every advantage of a middle-class home, she never adapted to the conventions of the society around her. Despite a father who was active in public life and a mother known for her charm and sociability, Gertrud grew to be a solemn, introverted child. She disdained all fashion and luxury, had no interest in fine clothes, and avoided the usual girlish preoccupations. "I would have liked to be a Spartan," she later wrote. She seldom played with other children, preferring instead to inhabit a world of her own during solitary hours spent with books and nature. The large yard behind her parents' home, with its miniature "forest," its flowers, animals and birds, must have supplied her with many early impressions. Often she would close herself up in her room and read for hours. History fascinated her, and she delved into accounts of ancient civilizations and the cultures of the East. The period of the French Revolution preoccupied her too, and her walls were hung with pictures of Napoleon. In a large wooden chest she collected countless newspaper clippings on events that aroused her concern. And at an early age she began to write—exactly when, no one knows, for her poetry was a secret she seldom revealed to her family.

Seeming to prefigure her entire life, the youth of Gertrud Kolmar was "uneventful." To an outsider her early years must have resembled those she later attributed to Martha, the heroine of her short novel *Eine Mutter*: "With hardly a word she swept the floors, sat at the sewing machine, spent her free time with a book, or walked an hour or two alone through distant streets. In summer weather she might also sit in a park with her parents, and then perhaps would walk over to the station and gaze up with strange eyes at the elevated trains as they traveled in and out. Thus she reached her late twenties and knew precious little of what people call experience." [1]

Young Gertrud's education was thorough and conventional. She attended the local grammar school in Berlin-Westend and was later enrolled in the *Höhere Mädchenschule Klockow* (a private, girl's high school) from which she was graduated in 1911. Then, at the age of sixteen, she was sent away from Berlin for the first time to attend a home-economics school for women located on a farm near Leipzig. On completing this course she returned to Berlin and entered a teacher training seminar for language instructors, from which she emerged with diplomas in English and French. These two languages, and especially the latter, were to remain an important part of her life. She read widely in both, spoke them fluently, and through them gained vital inspiration for her work. It was perhaps largely through her knowledge of French and English (and of Russian, which she learned from a friend) that Gertrud Kolmar was able to develop a German poetic idiom so independent of the trends, traditions and "schools" of German literature.

The First World War came in 1914 and with it began a new phase in her life. During the next four years she was able to put her linguistic abilities to use at the prisoner-of-war compound Döberitz in Berlin, where she was employed as an interpreter and a postal censor.

More importantly, the war years were a fruitful period for her poetry. By 1917 she had written so many poems that her father decided that a few of them deserved to be published. In the fall of that year he secretly brought a portion of his daughter's work to his friend Fritz Cohn, manager of the Egon Fleischel publishing house, and by Christmas a thin, seventy-two page volume (*Gedichte*) appeared, the first to bear the pen name Gertrud Kolmar. The poems of this first collection betray the youth of their author, and are of little enduring value. Yet they also reveal many characteristics of the mature poet: her preference for large poem cycles, her adherence to traditional form, and her intense concern with the quintessential truths of a woman's life. The forty poems of the volume (most in the conventional mold of folksong, with strict rhyme and meter) are divided into three cycles entitled "Mother and Child," "Man and Woman," "Time and Eternity." Amidst the harmless romanticisms that characterize most of these early poems we find some darker tones that foreshadow the poetic images and real events to come:

> Pain stands along the road I want to travel,
> Death stands along the road I want to travel,
> Sorrow and lament and somber torment.
> This I know—but still I travel on! [2]

Of all the events during the War, however, none was of greater consequence to Gertrud Kolmar than her first love affair. Not much is known about this encounter except what little her sister Hilde later revealed in these circumspect terms: "At the beginning of the First World War Gertrud met the man to whom, with all the unlimited sincerity of her ardent heart, she gave everything—only then (young and inexperienced as she was) to be bitterly disappointed." [3] This may seem inconsequential enough to us today: an event eternally recurring in the lives of countless young girls. But to Gertrud Kolmar it appears to have been the one truly great event of her life, her "year zero," the axial point around which all her later spiritual life was to revolve. It was Gertrud Kolmar's great gift—perhaps even the key to her poetic genius—that she was able to store up a few great emotional experiences and draw strength and inspiration from them for years to come. Only this faculty can account for the extraordinary fact that she—who had so few "actual" experiences with love, who never married and never bore a child—was able to produce some of the most powerful poems on female sexuality, love, and motherhood ever written. Late in her life, in one of the last letters to her sister, she remarked on this phenomenon of the "heart's memory": "I assume that many women have been granted an intense love experience; why doesn't this bright ceremony shine deeper into their everyday lives? Can't a treasure gathered at twenty endure until forty? . . . And why do the splendors of a love which reached the height of happiness—the lasting union of two lovers—disappear sooner from the heart's memory than the thought of a passing dispute?" [4]

In another letter she resorts to metaphor to illustrate the lasting effect of her early love: "I was never one of those who collect many smaller joys to make a larger happiness as though putting together a bouquet of flowers. For me there had to be the one great ecstasy, the perfect happiness, a sun which then poured forth its rays of lesser delights. This sun may at times be clouded over, shrouded in fog, hidden by night; yet I know that it remains there, steadfast—a fixed star and not a wandering planet." [5]

All we know of Gertrud's lover are his initials: "K. J.", found in the dedications to a few poems. A later work entitled "The Abandoned Woman" is one of these, and it contains the following lines:

> You're wrong. Do you believe that you are far away,
> And that I thirst and cannot find you? . . .
>
> How will you hope to leave my senses,
> The hunting snare from which no beast escapes? [6]

One of her finest sonnets, "Love," which is dedicated to the memory of K. J., strikes a more sorrowful chord in its closing sestet:

> A steady flame, oh light, you disappear;
> Thus, little boat, you sink without a cry.
> I hear your silence; grief I cannot hear.
>
> I look at you and watch the earth roll by.
> Now that you've gone, my summer day, my dear,
> I live that I may mourn to see you die.[7]

In 1918, still in the shadow of her lost love, Gertrud Kolmar wrote her first historical poem cycle, *Napoleon und Marie.* This sequence of nineteen poems is clear evidence of the capacity for self-transformation (*Verwandlung*) that she later developed to such a remarkable degree in her mature work. Just as, in her later poems, she was able to "become" a witch, an elk, or even a continent, in *Napoleon und Marie* she transforms herself into Marie Walewska, the Polish countess who was loved and abandoned by Napoleon. Thus she was able to idealize her own ill-fated love affair as well as express her enthusiastic, almost Gallic admiration for Napoleon. The poems themselves, while they exhibit greater formal variety and stronger imagery than those of the 1917 volume, are still far from esthetically satisfying. Only a few point toward the greater work to come. The last poem in the cycle is a good example of Kolmaresque *Verwandlung*, as Marie imagines herself a sleighbell on the horse that draws the defeated Bonaparte away from Moscow. This poem also suggests that Gertrud Kolmar's spiritual identification with the East—so evident in her later work—may well date back to her youth:

SOMEWHERE IN RUSSIA

Somewhere in Russia is my soul.

Somewhere in Russia
The storm sends snow into his coat,
A small bell cries
On the harness of the horse that pulls the sleigh.
It is my soul.
Somewhere in Russia
A raven flies over white, white fields,
My tired eagle
Drags his broken wing.
Behind his heavy breathing
Long across white fields
Trails a track of blood.[8]

Early in the 1920s she began to devote herself to another great love in her life: children. Few poets have expressed a more obsessive love and concern for children than did Gertrud Kolmar, who was destined never to be a mother. But this concern was not limited to her inner, poetic life.

Unwilling to begin a convenient career as a language teacher, Gertrud chose instead to devote herself to the education of children, especially those with handicaps. Throughout the twenties and thirties, whenever she was free of duties to her family, she was active as a teacher of deaf-mute children and as a tutor in private homes. Her last preserved work, the story *Susanna* from the year 1940, is written from the perspective of just such a teacher.

The summer of 1923 brought an important change in Gertrud's life. It was then that her family moved its residence from the comfortable but urban Berlin West to the distant rural suburb of Finkenkrug. It was here that she spent a great deal of the next fifteen years—serving her family and creating all of her truly significant poetry. In Finkenkrug Gertrud was for the first time close to nature, and it was only here that she seems to have felt at home. Here she grew to love the green landscape of the Mark Brandenburg and became the friend of flowers and trees and animals. As her many animal poems testify, she had a special fondness for the smaller, less favored creatures, such as insects, lizards and toads that inhabited her garden. Perhaps most of all she loved her dog, a Russian wolfhound named Flora, who accompanied her on many walks through the lanes and fields near her home:

On autumn nights
When strong, colder stars are sparkling,
And now and then a drop falls from a tree,
When yellowed grass breathes fresh and damp,
I pull my coat around my shoulders,
Open up the garden's iron gate;
You race with giant bounds.
You fly, you drive
Like a snowstorm across the carpet of wilted,
dripping leaves.[9]

Years later, after she was forced (by anti-Semitic decree) to leave this home, she spoke of it in letters as her "lost paradise": "I grew homesick for Finkenkrug. Not that I liked the people there. On the contrary. But the meadows, the forest and the 'new lot!' . . . And the animals—Flora! If only once I could brush and comb her again . . . Will I ever find this 'lost paradise' again?" [10] And in another letter she reveals the true meaning Finkenkrug had for her, and why such a place was so essential to her poetry: "Perhaps it is not Finkenkrug itself that I miss, but something eternal, plants and animals, the ever-returning, that which is constant in its growing and passing away." [11]

It was probably during her first years at Finkenkrug that she completed the three extended lyric cycles, selections from which appear under the heading "Early Poems" in the 1960 edition of her collected verse. Though most of these poems are of no great weight, a few, probably written around 1925, seem to open the door to an entirely new poetic vision and vocabulary, and bear the unmistakable mark of her best mature work:

Berry Pickers

Poor, ugly women dressed in manycolored rags,
Here too they pick their berries, seek and break the twigs,
And yet these woods are full of miracles,
And no more signposts mark the roads.

But boundary stones persist, great hunchbacked blocks,
Like stocky gnomes with grayish, weatherbeaten faces.
White pebbles lie transparent, filled with threadlike
veins of blood.
The evening finds a strange, dead, uniformly muted light.

Behind a crashing shower a colored double arch is built:
Two rainbows rising from the valley's houses.

Lightning flashes bright; and so the town looks
commonplace again.
The sky is drawn across it by a formless hand.

Huge frogs with lemon-yellow breasts lurk deep in caves,
Bilberries ripen, some as large as grapes,
The day's blue sky roars like the surf on wooded coasts,
And stars pass through the night like naked girls
through moss.[12]

Unprecedented here is the powerful presence of nature: evidence of the profound effect of a new sensory environment. Gertrud was forever after to remain at least to some degree a "nature poet." But her poems of the natural world, like "Berry Pickers," are no mere descriptions of landscapes, plants and animals. Nor is nature simply a decorative backdrop or a mirror for her own emotional states. As in the best later work of German nature poets such as Huchel, Eich, and Bobrowski, Gertrud Kolmar's natural world has a mysterious life of its own. It is filled with hidden meaning (the signposts, boundary stones, pebbles, rainbows, etc.), and, though alien to man, exists as an eternal presence that surrounds and overshadows his world (the berry pickers, the town). The metaphors of these early verses are remarkable for their boldness (border stones as gnomes, stars as naked girls) and for the way they bring the inanimate to life. "Berry Pickers" is also an early example of Gertrud Kolmar's innate "sensualism"—in the strong, sometimes almost tactile visual images, the colors, the intense lights and darks, and the synesthesia of the penultimate line. Perhaps most typical of her later work are the beasts: the giant, cave-dwelling frogs in the last stanza. An abundance of such strange, burrowing creatures populates her mature poems, where they hide like termites in rotten wood, symbols of some mysterious vital force that lives beneath the surface of things.

1927 was Gertrud's year to "see the world." And it was the last time she was to spend an extended period away from her parents and the environs of Berlin. She first took a job as a private tutor in Peine near Braunschweig, and then, early in 1927, moved to a similar position in a private home in Hamburg. The latter city, with its promenades along the water, its church steeples, and its harbor full of ocean-going ships, impressed her greatly: "I remember one evening fishing for smelt, and the 'Kap Polonio' lay there with its red-banded smokestacks . . . And the canals, and the gilded spire of the St. Petri tower . . . and the city park and the botanical garden, and the great houses of Harvesthude, whose lawns in early spring are buried under wood hyacinths and crocuses . . . And the gulls on the Jungfernstieg . . . All that and more my memory preserves as a gallery of beautiful pictures." [13] Such memories are also brought to life in her late poem "The City," where she describes a pair of lovers strolling through the fog of a cold spring morning in Hamburg:

They strode past frosty lawns and the ivy-covered columns
of closed gardens.
When they reached the long stone bridge
The sun threw off its robe of fog
And the city rose up steep behind the widespread basin of the river.
Roofs stood shuffled, stacked upon each other, shining blackish gray like jackdaws' feathers, some with green patina rising higher; golden hoods of towers gleamed.
Circling seagulls screamed, hungry flapping beggars, 'round the bridge's railing.[14]

Most of all it was the romance of the sea that so affected Gertrud Kolmar about Hamburg and the other North German cities that she visited. And in all her later work we find her using powerful "marine" images: oceans, beaches, ships, and exotic varieties of undersea flora and fauna. Such references to the sea are especially common in passages with a strong erotic context:

> With my goldbrown eyes I'll catch my prey,
> Catch the fish in ditches dug in clay,
> Catch the fish at sea; and the sea is wide and old,
> With broken masts and sunken chests of gold.[15]

Among the most remarkable of such passages is her dreamlike portrayal, in *Eine Mutter*, of Martha's semi-nude walk through the pouring rain on a summer night in Berlin: "She strode through halls of dusky seas, rolling, surging and murmuring, with flowing shadows of giant plants that grew out of the ocean floor and bellies of ships that sailed away over her head. Beards of seaweed were thickly tangled around drowned planks. Her foot trod muddy sand." [16]

Sometimes she describes a phantom lover—half-incubus, half-merman—who leaves the sea at night to visit her. He is the "fish king" of her poem of that title dedicated to the long lost K. J.,[17] or the "sea king" described in her last story by the girl Susanna: "Do you know what the Sea King is like? His chest is covered with a bushy pelt of black-green seaweed, and his head is round and polished smooth as the stones on the beach. And he wears as a crown two silver fish that bite each other's tails. . . . I will go to sleep and wait for the Sea King. He only comes at night." [18]

And most memorable of all is the "Sea Monster" of Gertrud Kolmar's greatest love poem:

> At midnight you had risen from the sea,
> Your body dripping cool and icy smooth.
> The ocean spoke a hushed soliloquy
> Of how you lay so gently next to me
> And how your arms embraced and soothed.

Sea-virgins came and swam mysterious dances;
Dark music from wild harps resounded free.
The moon poured out its light in silvery lances
On pearly scales and submarine romances;
And all my sheets smelled of the sea.[19]

This latter poem forms the concluding piece to what Gertrud Kolmar called her "travel diary": a cycle of seven poems (written some years after 1927) commemorating her journey to Hamburg, Lübeck and Travemünde. These she must have hoped to publish as a separate cycle, under the pretense that they were translations from English, for among her manuscripts we find the following title page: "Sieben Gedichte aus 'German Sea' von Helen Lodgers/ Nach dem Englischen/Leda/On the Alster/Nights/ Watching Thy Sleep . . . /The Worshipful Company of Seafaring Men/Travemuende/Sea-Monster."[20]

The thing perhaps most extraordinary about these poems, and the many others whose images show the same strong influence of the sea, is that they were inspired by an experience of such short duration. Her stay in Hamburg lasted only a few months, and in the summer of 1927 she departed for Dijon, France. During this first and only sojourn beyond the borders of Germany, Gertrud attended a short course at the University of Dijon, was awarded a diploma, traveled to Paris, and in general strengthened her already close ties to France. Once again she was able to make use of her gift for languages, and (as her sister reports) she was sometimes taken for a born *Parisienne.* And there can be no doubt that this journey, like every other intense experience in her life, was a major stimulus to her poetry. The influence of French history (Napoleon, Robespierre) and French literature (from Leconte de Lisle to Julian Green) is evident in her writing, but it is impossible to say how much of this was the result of her studies or literary encounters while in France. Certain direct experiences from her French tour are, however, traceable in her poetry—such as the encounter with a mad woman, which she recounts ("transformed" to the woman herself) in the poem "Die Irre," subtitled "Beaune, Côte d'Or, den 14.10.1927."

But the best evidence of the productive inspiration of her travels in 1927 are the works she produced immediately thereafter. Having returned to Berlin late in the year, Gertrud Kolmar began her first of several periods of prodigious creative activity. In the single winter of 1927–1928 she created the long sequence of poems *Alte Stadtwappen* (*Old City Coats of Arms*)—her first truly important work. Eighteen of these poems were published during her lifetime in the collection *Preussische Wappen* (*Prussian Coats of Arms*). Although the book did not appear until 1934, an author's note reveals that the poems were written "in the winter of 1927/28." Whether or not the entire group of fifty-three *Alte Stadtwappen* were completed at this time is uncertain, though it is quite possible in view of the stylistic qualities shared by all the poems.

What a surprising contrast there is between one's expectations upon reading the words "coats of arms" and an actual encounter with the poems! Where one might expect a patriotic tribute to German history or a poetic reflection on provincial cities, one finds scarcely a reference to "actual" events and hardly a mention of cities. These poems show small concern for the world of civilized men—except as it threatens the natural world. They are hymns of praise to the elements, reflections on the eternal truths of life—birth, love, and death, or more often, elegies to a Creation doomed to extinction in the face of human "progress."

Gertrud Kolmar had no interest in heraldry. And her purpose, certainly, was not to revive the emblem literature of the seventeenth century (though it is tempting to draw such parallels). The coats of arms she describes in a few words before each poem were found—not in scholarly reference books—but on packages of *Kaffee Haag*, a brand of coffee popular in Germany during the twenties. What fascinated her about these heraldic shields was the purity and the symbolic potency of their images. Castles, flowers, stars, suns, moons, trees, and above all animals—these became for Gertrud Kolmar the abstract signs of an eternal, elemental world. With inexhaustible, sometimes logic-defying imagination, she transforms these simple emblems into intricate poetic visions. The shield of Elmshorn, for example ("On red, over waves, an old-fashioned, silver sailing ship"), becomes a token of motherhood:

> Our mother forges through the seas,
> And prays with masts to ward off harm,
> For lucky stars, a gentle breeze,
> With saintly, outstretched, woman's arms.[21]

And the arms of Frauenburg (a castle with a praying woman on its central turret) come to symbolize the "eternal woman," imprisoned in her role of mediator between time and eternity, forever detached from the tumult of world events that rages beneath her fortress. The climbing silver fish against a starry sky in the emblem of Lassan represents —far from any Christian implications—a kind of spiritual transcendence that men and women are allowed to sense on rare occasions. Such animal images are more numerous than any others in these poems, and provide evidence of Gertrud Kolmar's intense love for animals, and of her almost archaic response to them as quasi-religious symbols. The elk in the shield of Allenburg stands for all the animals that man threatens with extinction:

> I am what was, the far departed age
> That, wild, in giant wooded moors once housed,
> That blew the wolves along when blizzards raged,
> And, dark with storms, the sleeping owls once roused.

I am the dumb, the wild, the things now dead
That men have killed for being mute and strange,
That dragged the heavy plow and spurred the sled,
Adorned by murderers with charming chains.[22]

And as the emblem of Usedom we find a mythical creature, a "Fischgreif," half-griffon, half-fish, transformed into a symbol of some great, sinister fatality—a beast god whose sacrificial death spells doom for man:

And when, upon the altar, I must die,
Because the beast is weak and man too small,
And send the universe a silent cry,
Eternal worlds will echo back my call.
And when I bend my neck
The shaking earth will wreck
Its cities: I am greatest. I am all.[23]

From the time when the *Alte Stadtwappen* were composed (in her thirty-second and thirty-third years) until her death sixteen years later, Gertrud Kolmar wrote poetry of consistently high quality. And throughout these years of her mature work, and seemingly to its advantage, her life remained outwardly uneventful. Until the end she lived in her parents' home, where she assumed the responsibility of caring for them in sickness and old age, spending long hours performing such common domestic tasks as cleaning, sewing, cooking, and gardening. Apparently she never resented these duties (cf. her splendid poem "Dienen" from the cycle *Welten*, where cooking takes on mythological dimensions), duties of the successful wife and mother she, at times, so longed to be, but never became.

In the year 1930 her mother died after a long illness, leaving Gertrud as sole housekeeper and companion to her sixty-nine-year-old father. Also in 1930 she published two poems in the yearbook of the Insel publishing house, "Die Gauklerin" ("The Woman Magician") and "Die Entführte" ("The Abducted Woman")—her first poems in print since the 1917 volume. The poems prove that she was, even then, working on the greatest of all her cycles, *Weibliches Bildnis* (*Image of Woman*), a task which seems to have preoccupied her for nearly ten years.

If Gertrud Kolmar succeeds in establishing a permanent literary reputation, this reputation will be based largely on the three cycles *Weibliches Bildnis*, *Kind* (*Child*), and *Tierträume* (*Animal Dreams*). With the exception of a few examples from the late collection *Welten*, the poems in these three cycles are her greatest. And more than any other portion of her work they serve to define her identity as a poet. Had all her other works but these been lost, our image of Gertrud Kolmar would remain essentially unchanged. She would remain the poet of "woman and animals," the title she gave to the last publication of her verse during her lifetime (*Die Frau und die Tiere*, Berlin, 1938), a collection drawn exclusively from the three cycles in question. All three share a common period of composition (from approximately 1928 to 1937) and a common, rather conservative approach to form. The majority of the poems are long (twenty lines or more) and constructed of stanzas containing four lines in common meters (four to six beats per line), usually with alternating end rhymes. Within the three cycles we also find the full range of Gertrud Kolmar's thematic concerns, nearly all of which circle incessantly around the primal image of woman.

The seventy-five poems of *Weibliches Bildnis* (*Image of Woman* or *Female Portrait*) are divided into four "rooms" or "spaces," an indication of the author's will to see her work in terms of concrete, three-dimensional reality. The poems of each room have only a loose thematic interconnection, but all are specifically concerned with one subject: woman in her many ages, roles and symbolic transformations.

Remarkably, every one of these poems is written in the first person, a testimony to Gertrud Kolmar's intense desire to personally identify with the many varieties of women she portrays. In the first room of the cycle we are introduced to the poet and to all her exotic worlds of metamorphosis. The poem titles, here and in the other rooms, are for the most part feminine nouns, imaginative names for the myriad reincarnations of woman: "The Traveling Woman," "The Witch," "The Robber Girl," "The Woman Tramp," "The Mother," "The Gardener," "The Lover," "The Abducted Woman," "The Sea Spirit." The second room is devoted primarily to the young woman, her attractiveness, and her erotic desires. The third emphasizes the mature lover (with the love poems from Hamburg and Travemünde), the sufferer, the Jew, and the woman bereaved of her child. The fourth and final room presents woman facing old age and death.

In the poems of *Weibliches Bildnis* we can already discern the five major transformations of the "lyric self" that characterize Gertrud Kolmar's poetry. In all of these transformations we see Gertrud Kolmar as a woman in love. She is a lover of the earth, of her people, of animals, of men, and of children—often tragically aware that she must lose the things she loves.

The first poetic metamorphosis reveals woman as a geographical presence, a mythical entity of gargantuan proportions:

> I will rest on my bed and cover the earth.
> Over the lands of Europe and Africa I lie,
> My left arm reaching deep into Asia,
> And the right towards America.
> My snaking hair will frighten the auk in Arctic seas.[24]

In thus identifying with the enormity of earth itself (a gesture reminiscent of the expansive ego of Walt Whitman)

Gertrud Kolmar does more than monumentalize woman as a kind of "earth mother," closely linked to the elements. The earth, with its many forms of terrain, its hidden treasures, its plants and animals, things seen and unseen, becomes symbolic of the immutable physical presence of woman and the infinite variety of her spiritual secrets:

> I too am a continent.
> I have unexplored mountains, bushland impenetrable
> and lost,
> Bays, stream-deltas, salt-licking tongues of coast,
> Caves where giant crawling beasts gleam dusky green,
> And inland seas where lemon-yellow jellyfish are seen.[25]

But the "terrestrial woman," like all of Gertrud Kolmar's other metamorphoses of the eternal feminine, also has its negative or tragic dimension:

> I am a continent that one day soon will sink without a sound
> into the sea.[26]

In another transformation Gertrud Kolmar presents woman—in each case one must almost say: herself—as an historical presence. She is the Jew, who, along with her people, endures through the ages despite unceasing persecution:

> Now I seem strange, no longer know myself,
> For I was there before great Rome and Carthage were,
> Because in me the altar fires ignite
> Of Deborah and her tribe.[27]

Gertrud Kolmar's love for the Jewish people was matched by her anguish over their persecution at the hands of the Nazis. One of her finest poems, "Wir Juden" ("We Jews") gives eloquent testimony to her compassion for her people, and, despite her powerlessness, her enormous desire to help:

And when your throat is gagged, your bleeding cry suppressed,
When brutal shackles bind your trembling arms,
Oh let me be the voice that echoes down the shaft of all eternity,
The hand stretched high to touch God's towering heaven.[28]

As if the suffering of the moment were not enough, she feels the crushing weight of all the injustices the Jews have suffered throughout history:

And we, we have proceeded through the gallows and the rack.

This bursting of our hearts, this sweat of death, this gaze
without a tear,
And the eternal windblown sigh of martyrs at the stake,
The withered claw, the weary fist with veins like vipers
Raised against the murderers from ropes and funeral pyres of
ages,

The gray beard singed in hellfires, torn by devils-grip,
The mutilated ear, the wounded brow and fleeing eye:
Oh all of you! Now, when the bitter hour strikes I will arise
And stand like a triumphal arch above your cavalcade of
anguish! [29]

At the same time she is always aware of the imminent threat to her own existence, and, in one moving line, can prophecy her own doom:

And I can feel the fist that drags my weeping head toward
the hill of ashes.[30]

But despite all this she is able to transcend the current suffering to see, in the very history of their persecution, a hope for the Jewish people. "God lets them fall in ruin," she says of the towers symbolizing her heritage, "and yet they stand for ages more." [31] In the long perspective of history, the endurance of her ancient people will prove itself again:

> For one day your weary wandering shoes will stand upon the
> necks of all the mighty! [32]

In *Weibliches Bildnis* (and most certainly in *Tierträume*) we find ample evidence of a third transformation: Gertrud Kolmar's close identification with animals. Not all the countless animals in her poems serve, of course, to receive the poet's identity. But many do, and when, in her poetry, she chooses to inhabit the form of a beast, it is usually for one of two reasons. In the first of these transformations she seeks to potentiate her female sexuality by linking it with the elemental ferocity of animals:

> A bat, I hang down rigid from a rafter,
> Drop free and catch your scent and follow after.
> Oh, man, I dream your blood; my bite is death.
> I'll claw into your hair and suck your breath.[33]

Elsewhere, she identifies with animals as creatures mistreated and exterminated by man:

> Alive you call us game or cattle; dead, a catch of meat—
> You grant us not an ocean drop, no grain of earth to keep.
> You pass away with heaven and hell; when we die off we're trash.
> And when we die, your one regret: we can't be killed again.
>
> But once I gave my images to you, to which you prayed,
> Until you found a human god, no longer god of beasts,
> And my descendants then were killed, my spring walled in with
> stone,
> And you called Holy Writ the things dictated you by greed.

And you have hope and pride, and a reward for all your pain,
An afterlife where you can safely flee into your soul.
But I endure a thousandfold in feathered cloaks and scales.
I am the carpet, when you weep, on which your sorrow kneels.[34]

The most important of Gertrud Kolmar's metamorphoses are those dealing specifically with woman. Often, and especially in *Weibliches Bildnis*, we encounter poems depicting woman in her fourth transformation, as lover. One of the most extraordinary aspects of Gertrud Kolmar's work is the unprecedented frankness and intensity of her portrayal of female sexuality. This is especially remarkable when one considers that Gertrud Kolmar was born in the nineteenth century and was surrounded by a taboo-ridden bourgeois moral code that barely admitted the existence of sexual needs in women. Since it is also known that she was a model of reserve and decorum in her personal life, it is all the more remarkable that she was able to inject such furious power—"elevated," to be sure, to a high plane of poetic art—into her evocations of sexual desire. These poems, with their potent concrete imagery, present severe, sometimes almost brutal views of a sexuality far from any cliché-norms of "feminine" delicacy and discretion:

Nude, I crouch on taloned toes
Sharpened red on rended meat;
In the reeds of swampy groves
I hide hunted and in heat.
Vipers wriggle through my fingers,
Snails wet my hair with slime,
And around my loins there linger
Colored toads of many kinds.

Tearing teeth crack brittle bones,
Crusted stems and hardened seeds.
Suddenly, with howling moans

Out I leap from mud and weeds,
Claws and body dragging down
A wanderer who lost his way.
Breast and flanks force to the ground . . .
Gasping, I devour my prey.[35]

When, at times, these expressions of erotic desire become still more intense, they reach a stage the poet Karl Krolow has called "menadic madness":

You. I want to wake you in the waters!
You. I want to melt you from the stars!
You. I want to lick you from the earth,
A bitch! And bite you out of fruit,
A savage! You. I want so much—
Dear. Dearest. Can't you give yourself to me?
And spend the blossoms, white,
Atop your flowering stem?[36]

But such bacchantic states are short-lived, and at other times there is a kind of remorse, or better, a tragic awareness of her helpless subjection to her own erotic nature, accompanied by the affirmation of an inner "chastity" that allows her soul, despite its passion, to "chant the psalms":

All that is true. I am not sinful, am not evil,
Do not steal the manhood of the dead or stab the childlike
eyes of birds,
Or break the trusting infant's tender spine.
I gnaw myself away in burning cries: oh set me free!

I am as martyrs burning at the stake, devoured
by snapping fangs
A woman, mate and mother, pregnant womb.

Above all those who now beget and are begotten blazes my
eternal heart.
And yet my soul kneels down and chants the psalms.[37]

And finally, among the many lovers in *Weibliches Bildnis* there is the woman forsaken by the man she loved, as in the poem "The Abandoned Woman," which has already been quoted above.

Woman's fifth and final transformation in the poems of *Weibliches Bildnis* is as a mother: often an imaginary one, and always a mother threatened with the loss of her beloved child—as is strikingly illustrated in the poem "Murder." [38] This most important of Gertrud Kolmar's poetic identities was given its own complete cycle entitled *Kind.*

In many respects the poems of *Kind (Child)* can be considered an extension of *Weibliches Bildnis.* Although few of the *Kind* poems use the feminine noun titles characteristic of the other cycle, most share the same approach to form, style, and first person perspective. And these poems too present "female portraits," only this time they are portraits exclusively of woman as mother. The evidence of this cycle alone would be enough to establish beyond doubt Gertrud Kolmar's obsessive concern for her own potential motherhood. It is a tragic concern, for although some of the poems could conceivably have been written by an actual mother about her own real children, most betray the author's painful awareness that her only children are offspring of the imagination:

My words are mad. My darkness calls you to me.
For in all my days you never were.[39]

These poems of unachieved motherhood are sometimes little more than desperate cries for the fulfillment she knows to be impossible:

Oh come.
My child. Oh come, oh come my child.
Oh come.
My hollow drumbeat deadens me no more.[40]

Gertrud Kolmar's fantasies concerning childlessness might easily seem pathetic or even morbid were they not distilled into beautiful poetry:

The night outside the door, the cradle void.
And rocking it, a woman, pallid-faced,
With stringy hair as black and thick as tar.
And in her heart there gathers gray on gray.

She minds a babe perhaps already dead,
And nods toward a child she never bore;
It was so lovely, white, carnation pink
With silver strands within its flaxen hair.

The night stands inside, and the cradle void.
And rocking it, a woman, driven mad,
Who loosens silken hair like ocean waves
The somber blue of fragrant hyacinths.[41]

There can be little doubt that Gertrud Kolmar is one of the world's great writers of "animal poems." We need no further evidence of this than the forty-nine poems of the cycle *Tierträume (Animal Dreams).* Certainly no other German poet has devoted such poetic skill to the portrayal of so many wild creatures.[42] Even Rilke's unquestioned masterpieces from his *Neue Gedichte* ("Der Panther," "Die Gazelle," "Das Einhorn," "Papageien-Park," "Die Flamingos") are no match for the number and intensity of the Kolmar poems.[43] Unlike Rilke, she does not use animals merely as objects for metaphysical speculation. She is profoundly interested in the animals *themselves,* and is deeply compassionate with their suffering at the hands of men. A striking example of this concern is her long poem from *Tierträume* entitled "The Day of Accusation." [44] Here she presents an apocalyptic vision, a day of judgment for mankind, not at the hands of God, but by all the animals that men have tortured, mutilated and enslaved. Out of the earth and from the waters swarm the hordes of resurrected creatures, all bearing the marks of their suffering: flies without wings or legs, blinded birds, carps with bellies slashed. Out of laboratories stream dissected rats, disfigured mice; and the zoos release their multitudes of benumbed captives. All congregate in a gigantic open space where they pass final judgment on their oppressor:

> A thousand bodies showed him all their graves,
> A hundred thousand more their torture cells,
> No dove came soaring now to rescue him.
> No lamb appeared to hold the shepherd's staff.

Man's egocentric God has failed him, and in His place:

> There came a new God, dragonlike,
> That spat his flame toward a new horizon.

This awesome dragon-god at the poem's conclusion represents another vision of the animal found in *Tierträume.* The beast is not only a sufferer, he is the symbol of the mysterious forces of nature (as in "The Herons" or "Hyenas"). At times he takes the form of some indifferent power that drives the universe, a cruel "god" whose ways are beyond man's understanding or control. One example of such a "beast god" is the vulture in the poem of that name:

> As mad volcanoes spurt,
> Cold-sparkling glaciers slide,
> You clench the clods of dirt

Where anthill cities hide.
And when your blazing head
Looks down upon our earth,
No single tear is shed
Into the endless dearth.[45]

Only some of Gertrud Kolmar's mature work can be dated with any certainty. Much of her best poetry, including the sonnets, and the cycles *Weibliches Bildnis*, *Kind*, and *Tierträume* lack any precise indication as to their time of composition. Of these four series, however, the sonnets (first published posthumously) seem to have been completed earliest, and—judging from certain similarities to the novel *Eine Mutter* (1930–1931)—may well have been written at the beginning of the new decade.

Nineteen sonnets, plus one poem of another form, comprise the cycle *Bild der Rose (Image of the Rose)*. Aside from four other examples ("Wappen von Borkem" in *Alte Stadtwappen*, "Zwergkämpfer" from *Tierträume*, "Die Messe von Soissons" and "Marat Triumphator" from *Robespierre*) these poems are Gertrud Kolmar's only excursions into the form. But they are not such peculiar exceptions to the "usual" character of her work as might first be assumed. Indeed, it is not surprising that, despite her "elemental" imagination, she was able to discipline herself to the stringencies of sonnet form. Virtually all of her poetry—up to the late cycle *Welten*—is characterized by an almost obsessive concern for form: strict meters, regular rhyme schemes, and consistent patterns of line and stanza length. What is unusual about the rose sonnets is their relative brevity (for such an expansive writer, fourteen lines is short!), and their formal consistency, since her cycles usually consist of an enormous variety of structural patterns. Also unique are the obvious connections to French poetry of the nineteenth century, especially Baudelaire, Verlaine and Leconte de Lisle.

These sonnets resemble the *Stadtwappen* poems in that they are highly imaginative reflections on specific simple images: the roses of the Chodziesner garden, whose hybrid types (e.g., "Etoile de Hollande") are often named just beneath the titles. To Gertrud Kolmar, each rose becomes a symbol, a gateway to fantasy. Sometimes they are personified, and the rose (as well as the poet herself) is transformed into a mulatto girl ("Mulattenrose") or a maid of the tropics ("Orangengesicht") or a romantic *bourgeoise* ("Bürgerrose" or "Rose Chiffon"[46]) or an actress ("Schauspielerin"). Still others become birds ("Kanarienrose" and "Rose des Kondors"), a Chinese jacket ("Chinesische Rose"), a piece of marzipan ("Marzipanrose"), or a red lamp symbolizing Gertrud's love for the lost K. J. ("Liebe"). The introductory sonnet of the cycle ("Die schönen Wunder") shows perhaps best of all Gertrud Kolmar's attitude toward the roses as emotion-laden symbols of a magical vitality:

The fairest wonders from the seven zones,
That now are butterflies on stems that sway,
Now seashells out of magic silent bays,
Now dwarf-flamingoes set among the stones.

Oh you, my roses. Hearts. Though you be thrown
To earth by wilting, white-hot sunlight's rays,
Consumed with ecstasy in raging days,
Still hasten singing to the grave alone!

I will not cut you, will not make you tame,
Imprison you in narrow, tepid glass,
Nor will prolong the moment of your bloom.

Oh good: to burn in boundless, blinding flame,
And not be sundered from the earth and grass
To languish long within an empty room.[47]

In 1931 Gertrud Kolmar completed the longest and most intriguing of her few prose works, the short novel *Eine Mutter*.[48] Like all her attempts outside the medium of poetry, this book is not totally satisfying (owing to its lack of a confident and consistent prose style), but it contains several great passages and a wealth of fascinating insight about its author.

Eine Mutter, the story of a lonely woman of Berlin, is not without its autobiographical implications. The protagonist, Martha Jadassohn, is a Jewish girl of humble background. At an early age she is brought to Berlin by her parents, natives of a small town in western Poland. She grows up a withdrawn child, forever alien to her social environment, but full of pride and unshakable will. Reaching her late twenties without notable experience in the world, she meets the young engineer Friedrich Wolg, a Christian. He falls in love with her and they marry, despite his father's objections to her Jewishness ("She looks like someone out of the Old Testament.") and her cold solemnity ("Jerusalem at the North Pole").[49] The marriage is doomed from the start. Martha remains outwardly aloof from her husband; their relationship is almost completely sexual ("I have a lover, not a wife.").[50] A child is born, a daughter Ursula, who inherits all of her mother's "darkness" and none of her father's blond Germanic traits. "Like an animal mother," Martha virtually pounces on the child, and devotes her every energy to its care. Friedrich Wolg, almost completely shut out, abandons his wife and child just as his father had predicted. ("Either you will run away or she will break you in pieces.")[51]

Totally alone in the world (her parents had died), Martha resolves to raise the child by herself, living in the humble, almost proletarian milieu of a Berlin tenement, and working as a photographer. ("She showed her greatest talent in portraying animals.")[52] The mother loves her child intensely, but must leave her with a neighbor during working hours. Fears for the child's safety are one day confirmed when Martha returns to find Ursula missing. A long and agonizing search finally ends with Martha's discovery of her daughter lying near death in an abandoned shed, the victim of a brutal rape. The child is hospitalized, but barely clings to life. To end its misery, Martha secretly poisons the child, thus shouldering an enormous guilt from which she will never escape.

The remaining two-thirds of the novel are devoted to Martha's unrelenting search for revenge. She consults the police, lawyers, even a furtune-teller, but all in vain. At last she resolves to take a lover whom she can enlist in the search for the criminal who destroyed her child. After luring the man, Albert Renkens, into her bed, she implores the spirit of the dead child to understand. ("Ursa, I'm doing it for you!")[53] But it is clear that she needs Renkens, not only as a detective, but to satisfy her own profound sexual needs, now aggravated by years of loneliness. This becomes tragically evident when Renkens begins to feel trapped in the relationship and leaves her. Martha succeeds in locating him again and, vowing her love, pleads with him to return. He cannot. ("At night there was always this child's corpse between us.")[54] Totally humiliating herself, Martha promises to forget her child, tears Ursula's photograph to pieces, and finally, in desperation, admits to having committed the murder. This only alienates Renkens further. ("If anything separates us more sharply, it is that. . . . Please go. . . . I am afraid to hear any more of your confessions.")[55] Crushed by this rejection and overwhelmed by guilt, Martha, on a winter's night, drowns herself in the river Spree.

It is an unusual work, not without its stylistic quirks and banalities, but filled at times with a strange poetic force and a feverish emotional intensity unsurpassed in Gertrud Kolmar's work. This seminovel, this odd mixture of pulp romance, *Kriminalroman* and symbolic fairy tale is perhaps most remarkable as an expression of the harrowing child-loss fantasies that plagued the author throughout her life and find expression in so many of her poems.[56] Perhaps more than any other of her works, *Eine Mutter* provides the basis for a psychoanalytic interpretation: particularly in relation to the motifs of sexuality, motherhood, guilt and atonement, which reappear with obsessive regularity in her writing. The novel is a rich mine of evidence to use in defining the thematic currents running throughout her *oeuvre.* Here we find the archetypal woman—the core of Gertrud Kolmar's poetic vision—mythologized in all her transformations: from bacchantic lover, to mother, to animal, to historical presence. In these, Martha is monumentalized as the vampirelike lover, the she-wolf mother, the lonely elk threatened with extinction, the stone idol of an ancient goddess, or as the ageless symbol of Jewish womanhood.

But for all its timeless, mythological dimensions, *Eine Mutter* is also striking for its occasional reflection of the concrete realities of Berlin in the late 1920s. It is perhaps remarkable in itself, given her idyllic situation in Finkenkrug and her propensity for the foreign, the archaic and the eternal, that Gertrud Kolmar resisted the temptation to write an "exotic" novel set in some remote valley of time and space. But it is evident that the same sensitivities that helped her transcend the everyday, also responded to the pressing significance of current events. Thus in facing the metropolitan world of Berlin, she was able to deal with some of the threatening aspects of modern civilization (such as crime, bureaucracy, social alienation) as well as with the most urgent issue of all: rising German anti-Semitism.

In a passage near the end of *Eine Mutter* Martha encounters an example of the kind of vulgar anti-Jewish propaganda then current in Germany. The passage provides Gertrud Kolmar with an opportunity to comment on the danger facing her people: "The cover said: 'Hugin—Deutsche Wehr—Blätter für völkisches Denken,' and between the titles a raven held a swastika shield in its claws. She paged through it at random; she found what she was looking for. '. . . cunningly Juda has fashioned the yoke for Germanic necks.' 'The true enemy . . . passes by you every day, flatfooted, fat-bellied, hook-nosed, black.' 'The sons and daughters of Israel . . . parasitic plants on the German tree . . . ' . . . She lowered her head, read further: ' . . . and we still refuse to see it. Jewish arrogance . . . ' She thought: arrogance . . . ? We aren't arrogant, unfortunately not; but we could be. Yes, we have a right to be. We have outlived Rome and seen Byzantium in ruins; and now this enemy will only kill us if we destroy ourselves. We only must be strong and have the courage to sink again, to endure . . . We must go inside ourselves again; no one can pursue us there . . . 'Israel is like the dust of the earth: all tread upon it with their feet; but the dust outlives them all.' "[57]

Whereas the apocalyptic implications of these lines could still be considered a prophecy in 1931 (albeit one requiring little clairvoyance), the events of January 1933 made the question of Jewish destiny a matter of political inevitability. Hitler's assumption of power had a profound and immediate effect on the poet Gertrud Kolmar, the extent of which has only recently been learned. Thanks to the discovery in East Germany of her 1933 poem cycle *Das Wort der Stummen (Words of the Silent People)*,[58] we can see how intensely Gertrud Kolmar reacted to the Nazi takeover and how clearly she foresaw the human tragedy it implied. Only three of the cycle's new poems have been published.[59] And while these do not meet the high standards of her other poetry (the probable reason for their disappearance), they are moving testimony to the compassion and foresight of a poet whom some might have considered a dreamer or an esthetic escapist. In 1933, long before the *Kristallnacht* or the mass exterminations, she evokes the dreadful horror of the concentration camps in the poem "Im Lager" ("In the Camp"):

Those who walk about here are but bodies
And have no longer any soul,
Are only names in books,
Imprisoned: Men and boys and women,
And their eyes stare emptily.

With crumbling, ruined gazes
For hours when in a gloomy cell,
When strangled, trampled, beaten blind,
Their tortured groan, their fear insane,
A creature crept on hands and feet . . .

They all have ears and hear
No longer their own cries.
The prison walls press in, destroy:
No heart, no heart remains to rage!
The soft alarm-clock shrills until it breaks.

Insensate, gray, degenerate they toil,
Cut off from human life,
Stiff, wounded, branded with official stamps,
They wait like slaughter cattle for the knife,
And still remember dimly trough and herd.

And only fear remains, a trembling face,
When late at night a gunshot strikes its mark . . .
And no one sees the man appear
Who, silently, within their midst,
Conveys his barren cross towards the hill.[60]

During the period of 1933–1935 Gertrud Kolmar devoted herself, as never before or after, to history. Perhaps she sought in the historical perspective a solution to the political dilemmas of Germany under fascism, a solution unattainable through an introspective concentration on eternal values.

In the fall of 1933 she produced what, for a poet, must be considered a highly unusual work: a scholarly essay on the French revolutionary hero Robespierre (*Das Bildnis Robespierres*).[61] This essay, surprising in its erudition, can be viewed as an extension of her youthful interest in French history. It rectifies what Gertrud Kolmar felt to be distortions in the image of Robespierre presented by certain historians. But it is also a remarkable testimony of faith in revolution as a positive force in human history. Such a sentiment would hardly be very startling if expressed from a French perspective. But when one considers that the essay in question was written by a Jewish intellectual inside Nazi Germany it becomes difficult to see it as anything but a direct political statement. Consider this passage near the conclusion of the essay: "If Robespierre had set himself up, as if on a pedestal, upon the sarcophagus of the Revolution, people everywhere would call him a great man today. But instead, upon his corpse he stabilized the Revolution for centuries. That was hardly his achievement, his deed; that was his nature. People have accused him of 'not ending the Revolution,' of 'not closing the abyss of revolution.' No, he declared its permanence. By leaving it unfinished he allowed it to be resumed and carried further at any time. And the 'abyss of revolution?' He threw himself into it as a sacrifice, like Marcus Curtius, not to close it, but to keep it open." [62]

Gertrud Kolmar's interest in Robespierre was not exhausted by her work on the essay. After concluding it she wrote her second and last cycle of "historical" poems, *Robespierre.* These forty-five poems are similar to her "woman and animal" cycles in that they use a comparable approach to rhyme and meter and appear in a variety of forms, ranging from sonnets to long poems of nearly a hundred lines. Yet their thematic focus is quite different. Even despite Gertrud Kolmar's extremely subjective approach, despite her will to identify with the revolutionary heroes she describes, these poems still represent attempts to characterize objective historical situations. As such they depart from the approach she had used so successfully in nearly all her previous poetry. In *Robespierre* she abandons, if only for the moment, her pursuit of the truth about woman and nature, perhaps reminded of the irrelevance of such themes to the current political crisis. Yet the Robespierre poems, though in a sense "historical," are hardly more politically relevant than are her other poems—or, one might even venture to say, than are *any* poems. Hitler was not to be dealt with by literary means.

As it stands, the Robespierre poems are more memorable in detail than as a successful unit. Among the best is a poem describing Paris on the eve of the Revolution:

> Houses decorate
> Every festival with stony songs.
> Bridges strong and great
> Channel milling, motley-colored throngs.
> Trees along the moats
> Closed within the flowering arms of spring
> Smile on silent boats
> Rocked by gentle winds' gray whispering.
>
> Voids in gates are carved.
> Red-eyed windows stare like open graves.
> Withered bodies starve
> For food that holds them chained like shackled slaves.
> Heaven saves the dead—
> But down in some vile hell there swells and twists
> A serpent's head
> All black with veins, . . . a fist . . .[63]

During the winter of 1934–35 Gertrud Kolmar (now forty), still inspired by the subject of the French Revolution, wrote her first attempt in the dramatic genre, the historical play *Cécile Renault.* This drama, which shares many motifs and images with the Robespierre poems, has yet to be published.

But Gertrud Kolmar was not to continue her foray into history, for her next poems show a decisive return to her earlier thematic concerns. But these poems (*Welten*) were not written until late in 1937. For the period between March 1935 (conclusion of *Cécile Renault*), and August 1937 (beginning of work on *Welten*), we have no concrete indication of her creative activity. It is possible that she fell silent for a time, perhaps out of political frustration and resignation. But, more likely, she soon returned to her work on the cycles *Weibliches Bildnis*, *Kind*, and *Tierträume*, selections of which were to be published in 1938.

Whatever the significance of the apparent caesura between 1935 and 1937, one indisputable result of this period was a radical change in Gertrud Kolmar's poetic style. The poems of the cycle *Welten* (*Worlds*), written from August to December, 1937, represent a considerable departure from her earlier approach to form. These works, her last poetry to have been preserved, impress us most of all with their expansiveness. Her usual four-to-six beat line has grown, casting off all metrical regularity, and stretching to the extreme limit of what can be recited in a single breath (often twenty words and more). Interspersed among these far-reaching lines are contrasting short ones, sometimes no more than a word long, that serve as resting points for gathering the great energy to be expended in the long lines to follow. Rhyme, too, has been abandoned—of necessity—along with regular length of line.

The language of *Welten* is changed as well. Without rhythmic regularity and rhyme the poems show none of the qualities that typified her earlier verse: the tone of folksong or the sound of chanted liturgy or whispered magic charms. The new poems have lost all the former attributes of compression and cyclic formality. For once the outward form of Gertrud Kolmar's poetry appears to match its inner "elemental" drive. The sustained power of the language in *Welten*, and its elevated, sometimes almost scriptural dignity, is almost certainly patterned after the prose of the Old Testament. This is perhaps most evident in a poem based on an an explicitly Biblical theme such as "The Animals of Nineveh":

But Jonah went,
And the burden over Nineveh that he had seen, weighed on his head.
But he, in heavy brooding, strode away.—

A painted stone broke from the solid battlement atop the royal castle,
And there arose a howling and a shrieking in the storm, and then a voice cried out:
"For their sake!
For the sake of all the animals, clean and unclean!"
And the prophet of the Lord was frightened and looked up; but all was darkness and he heard no sound but ceaseless rush and roar
That grasped his robe and pulled and shook his garment like a pleading hand, as, merciless, he fled.
But he did not turn back; he traveled on
And close about him gathered up his robe.[64]

In a letter, Gertrud Kolmar herself admitted to this influence: "I have read Luther's Bible all my life, and people qualified to judge such things have said that its language has clearly influenced mine as a poet." [65]

There are seventeen poems in Gertrud Kolmar's last cycle, and each, in truth, contains its own "world." The poems are brimming with the "things of the earth," with the concrete images of sensory experience. These worlds are imaginary places of refuge from a harsh reality. Often they reflect the actual pleasures of her life at Finkenkrug, pleasures which, with her extraordinary ability to build on simple sense experiences, became exciting and exotic refuges for her soul: the garden ("Garten in Sommer"), the kitchen ("Dienen"), or walks through the surrounding countryside with her Russian wolfhound Flora ("Barzoi").

Other animals, besides the dog, are present too. Continuing her myth-making in the animal world she presents the unicorn (in "Das Einhorn") as a mysterious natural force with sexual overtones. In "The Animals of Nineveh" a cat, a dog, and a vulture are recipients of God's compassion along with a shepherd boy and a beggar child.

In other "worlds" Gertrud Kolmar reviews memories of her love affairs—real or imaginary ("Die Stadt," "Der Engel im Walde," "Sehnsucht"). And once again we encounter the transformations of woman: the menadic lover ("Sehnsucht"), the unfulfilled mother ("Fruchtlos"), the old woman remembering her lost love ("Die alte Frau"). The awareness of death fills these poems, and just as their worlds were a temporary refuge for the living poet, they also project the image of a permanent refuge for her soul:

> And now I stumble forward on the stony, stubborn path.
> Jumbled rocks and thistles wound my groping hands:
> A cave awaits me
> That conceals inside its deepest crack the bronze-green,
> nameless raven.
> I will enter
> And crouch down to rest beneath the sheltering shadows of
> his giant wings,
> And sleep, my brow turned eastward,
> 'Til the dawn.[66]

The protective towers of the poem "The Jewish Woman" (p. 109, below), symbolic of her ancient heritage, reappear to offer another possible sanctuary:

Perhaps my soul forgot me in my dream,
And sank, wings spread towards morning, where the tower
stood to meet its wandering flight,
And roved through hot, enchanted, lifeless rooms,
In search of ancestors,
And touched the hovering strings that still resound . . .[67]

The awareness of her coming death is also implicit in the poem "Das Opfer" ("The Sacrifice," p. 233, below), wherein she identifies with a woman of the Old Testament facing ritual sacrifice to a golden idol. But it is always to the East, to the expanses of Asia, that Gertrud Kolmar turns in search of a promised land to which she might escape. Again, as in her "geographical" transformation, she feels she can embrace the earth, here the Ural Mountains:

When I seize the darkness, rough crags
Wound my hand.[68]

Another refuge is the "Mergui Isles," a real island chain off Burma, which becomes a fantastic archipelago of dreams, a repository for all the secret visions that obsessed the poet:

My Mergui Isles do not bathe singing in the Indian Ocean.
They rise silently from seas of night into an ever-dayless twilight,
Domed and shaggy green and black,
The withers of some giant buffaloes that graze the brownish
seaweed from the ocean floor.[69]

No poem better expresses Gertrud Kolmar's longing for the life-transcending paradise of a visionary Asia than the last of the "worlds":

Mother,
Mine before my own had held me,
I am coming home.

Let me stand before you.
Let me sit in silence at your feet, and gazing up, discover you:
A proud, enshrouded figure rising mighty from your mythic
    throne
That rests upon the pillared feet of white stone elephants,
Its armrests jade-tongued dragons made of bronze.
I see your solemn, sun-gold face, spun round with silken,
    blue-black hair,
Your brow, the walled preserve of noble thoughts,
Your eyes, now gleaming dark obsidian,
Now deep and somber velvet jungle flowers.
Oh let me touch your robes that breathe the scent of amber trees
    and myrrh, of sandalwood and cinnamon,
Your flaming robes that blazed from Indian looms,
Your robes of pale corn-yellow that a Chinese girl embroidered
    with a brownish twig, an almond blossom and a small,
    rust-colored butterfly.
Show me your crowns: the southern one,
Green-golden leaves of palm, bedewed with pearls and mixed
    with blooming tourmaline and emerald and hyacinth and
    sapphire,
And the northern one that sparkles gems of ice and aquamarine
    droplets from Siberian seas.
Oh brush my forehead with your hand whose palm still holds the
    fragrant oil of Persian fruits,
And let the singing shawm play round my ear, as David's
    shepherd's pipe once sang across the meadows at Beth-
    Lechem.

At the end of this poem, the last one left to us by Gertrud Kolmar, the image of the towers returns once again. More enigmatic than before, this last religious vision declares her faith in the ancient "Asian" roots from which she sprang, and anticipates reunion with the mythical East, the eternal truth toward which she feels her soul directed:

. . . you have plunged down to the deepest center of our star, into
the foaming bath of fire . . .
Oh burn . . .
And hide in shame . . . your inmost secret that received the
flaming seed,
And let your progeny, the vulture-demons, circle endlessly above
the towers of death,
The towers of silence . . .[70]

1938 was to be a critical year for Gertrud Kolmar. In March her sister, Hilde Wenzel, succeeded in getting out of Germany and sought asylum in Switzerland. Not long thereafter Gertrud began an exchange of letters with her sister which was to last until the end. Besides providing us with a moving document of her last four years, this correspondence fulfilled an even more important function: it served as a bridge to the outside world over which Gertrud Kolmar was able to send many of her unpublished works to safety, among these the cycle *Welten* and the short story *Susanna.* One of the first works to be rescued in this way was her second play, a "dramatic legend" about the Roman emperor Tiberius entitled *Nacht* (*Night*), which was written between March and June of 1938. Like her first play, this work too remains unpublished.

Time was growing short for the Jews in Germany, and Gertrud's early letters reveal that she too planned to emigrate. In August 1938, she speaks, half-jokingly, of "training for Palestine," and in November mentions plans to go to England as a tutor. But none of these schemes were realized, primarily because of Gertrud's strong sense of duty to her father. Of all the four children of Ludwig Chodziesner, Gertrud alone remained to care for the old man, now aged seventy-seven.

In September, 1938, Gertrud witnessed the publication of her book *Die Frau und die Tiere* (*The Woman and the Animals*), and, for the first time in her life, experienced something which approached public recognition:

> Reviews have come out everywhere—often "very big" ones—whose authors admire and praise *Die Frau und die Tiere* even more unreservedly than the reporter of the *Central-Verein-Zeitung.*[71] Due to the conspicuousness of our name, these articles are being talked about all over town, and at times I have to think of Byron's comment: "I awoke one morning and found myself famous." (Of course, with me, things haven't gone quite so far yet!) But even when I am declared "the most important Jewish poetess since Else Lasker-Schüler," it makes father more happy than me; it doesn't excite me very much. There was a time when the praise of others could cheer me and urge me on (only I seldom looked for it and thus usually didn't get it); today I know, even without critics, what I am worth as a poet, what I can do and what I can't . . .[72]

But any pleasure over this recognition was short-lived indeed, and in the same letter she remarks: "In recent weeks it was always somehow difficult for me to read novels, even when they were good. Perhaps because now we are living some that put the written ones to shame." The "adventures" to which she so cautiously alludes[73] were, however, just beginning. On the night of the ninth to the tenth of November, 1938, occurred the hitherto greatest pogrom in German history, the *Kristallnacht.* In its wake the German Jews were subjected to increasing pressure by the Nazi authorities. All Jewish organizations were disbanded and their leaders arrested. The Jewish newspapers, which had so recently reviewed *Die Frau und die Tiere*, were ordered closed. Even the unsold copies of the volume itself were destroyed. A still greater blow to Gertrud Kolmar personally occurred on November 23 when she and her father were forced to sell the house in Finkenkrug because of new laws affecting Jewish property.

In January, 1939, Gertrud and her father finally left their beloved home and moved to an apartment which had been allocated to them in the central city of Berlin. The abrupt change of scene from the rural solitude of Finkenkrug to the ugliness of a downtown tenement district must have been disturbing indeed. After nearly five months in the city she confesses: "I am as much a stranger here as on the first day. . . . Perhaps I can no longer adjust to life in a large city, far from nature . . . Old trees shouldn't be transplanted." [74] The transition was especially destructive to her creative capacity: "This winter of moving has obviously done my Pegasus no good; but he will pick himself up again . . . and carry me on his back to a better land . . ." [75] Besides the alienating presence of the city, Gertrud had to contend with the severe restrictions now facing all Jews in Germany: exclusion from public entertainment and restriction from certain areas in Berlin. Soon it was impossible even to move about freely. Jews were prohibited from driving cars, could not ride public transportation (except to and from work as forced laborers), and finally could not even walk in parks or wooded areas. Not surprisingly, Gertrud's reaction to all this was to seek refuge within herself. In response to the radical transformations in her outward environment, she depended more and more on what she felt to be the certainties of life: " . . . what once took years or decades to change now requires only days. And in the meantime I have withdrawn deeper and deeper into permanence, into being, into the eternal process (this eternal process is not necessarily 'religion,' it can also be 'nature' or 'love') . . . " [76]

In December of 1939 Gertrud's "Pegasus" did indeed regain its feet, for it was then that she began work on the story *Susanna*, her last work to be saved for posterity. The story, which preoccupied her until February, 1940, was written under extremely unfavorable circumstances, forcing her to adopt a schedule reminiscent of Franz Kafka's *Manöver-Leben*:[77]

> I go to bed early, and when the tenants upstairs wake me with their usual very noisy homecoming between one and three o'clock, I have already slept a few hours and the "brainwork" can begin. When I have brought my "child" along a few more centimeters it is past five and I can doze a little while longer. In the morning after dressing I write everything down all at once; I'm very tired then, feel miserable, probably have a headache—in short all the signs of a "hangover" after a night of "excesses"—which, in reality, it was.[78]

This final volume in Gertrud Kolmar's *oeuvre* is a memorable piece of literature. In the ten years since the writing of *Eine Mutter* her prose style had assumed a temperate sureness and a convincing simplicity of means. Judging from this work alone it seems certain that, in Gertrud Kolmar, German literature lost a prose writer of potential greatness.

Susanna is the story of an aging private tutor who takes a job somewhere far in the German–Polish East in the household of the lawyer Fordon. He is the legal guardian of an adolescent girl (Susanna) who requires private care, apparently because of a mental disorder. The tutor arrives in the lonely town in the dead of winter, and is introduced to the strange girl. Susanna lives entirely in a world of fantasy. Her companion in this dream world is the Russian wolfhound Zoe, an almost ethereal beast, which the girl describes to her tutor as follows:

> She is a female and also a princess, empress of Byzantium. But she's not alive any more. She's called Zoe and lives in a very old century; which one I don't know. And now she's dead. And she only remains under the fur and in the eyes.

> But sometimes she flies off and stays away, and then the dog just sits there and stares and doesn't move and doesn't come when you call her. I heard a man tell her once: "Go on, you great ghost." The Empress of Byzantium married a lizard, that's how she got such a head. Once upon a time people and animals could marry; today they can't any more. I sometimes think whom I would have married ... perhaps a fish-hawk ... Or the Sea King; he sits under the waves in a glass house and climbs up onto the beach only at night when the moon shines, and has on his chest a tangle of seaweed like hair, and has greenish gray eyes.[79]

Unable (and, in truth, unwilling) to break the spell of this imaginary world, the tutor becomes Susanna's confidante. At home or during long walks through a memorably described winter landscape, Susanna initiates her new friend into her exotic, but totally consistent "mythology," wherein ordinary things and events became part of a fairy tale inhabited by strange people and animals. One strong element in this mythology is Susanna's unusual erotic interest in men. One night the tutor is witness to a rendezvous between Susanna and her "Sea King" lover, a young man from a nearby town. It is a totally innocent meeting at a window, but the tutor feels obliged to prevent the affair from developing further. Finally, she learns that the man himself has resolved to leave for Berlin, aware of the hopelessness of his love for the seductive, but "deranged" Susanna. The young girl learns of this, and writes him a last desperate letter. The message reaches not the young man but his mother, who, in an embarrassing and painful scene, confronts Susanna and her teacher—accusing the girl of lewdly tempting her son. The next morning Susanna is found to be missing, and is finally discovered lying dead along the railroad tracks leading to Berlin.

Soon after finishing *Susanna*, Gertrud Kolmar began work

on a second short story dealing with an imaginary island discovered by an eighteenth-century French explorer. But the project was short-lived: "... meanwhile, after I had populated the island with all sorts of plants and animals, it sank back into the sea ..." [80] Gertrud had not, however, abandoned the writing of poetry. In May of 1940 she began writing verse again, this time not in German, but in Hebrew! Her astonishing talent in languages had again proven itself: "... since the beginning of April, I have been taking Hebrew conversation—because a suitable teacher actually lives 'just around the corner.' She is giving such lessons, as she said, for the first time in twenty years because her previous students never got so far as to be able to carry on pure conversation. The successful result of this is that yesterday, on the 14th of May, after my fifth lesson, I 'committed' my first poem in Hebrew." [81]

Gertrud continued her Hebrew lessons and began to apply herself more seriously to writing poetry in the ancient language: "... recently I wrote another poem, for the first time one that is not just a curiosity . . . It is called 'Ha Tsav,' 'The Turtle' ... (My teacher) maintained that one line was stylistically quite innovative and worthy of Bialik.[82] She is a great admirer of Bialik and this is her highest praise." [83] In a letter of November 24, 1940, Gertrud reveals just how serious was her relationship to the Hebrew language and Hebrew poetry. She notes that her speaking ability has progressed to the extent that she plans to enter a discussion group for teachers of Hebrew. Also, she admits to having written several more poems that her teacher has declared worthy of publication. Then she embarks on a lengthy discussion of Hebrew poetry, which concludes:

> I have recently learned what a Hebrew poem should *not* be, and how I should not write, and feel now that I will soon know how I *must* write. This poem that does not yet exist ...

> is already forming within me. Perhaps it will take months or years . . . , but it will see the light. . . . Perhaps because of this I have written nothing more in German recently."

Unfortunately, no trace of Gertrud Kolmar's Hebrew poetry was saved.

Still greater hardship came to the life of Gertrud and her father in 1941. In May, following an official decree, they were forced to give over part of their apartment to new tenants. Slowly, in advance of deportation, all the Jews of Berlin were being herded together in a limited number of households. As a result of the increasingly unbearable situation at home, Gertrud was, it seems, almost relieved when she was called, in July, 1941, to enter forced labor in a factory in Berlin-Lichtenberg. Far from seeing this new burden as a ground for complaint, Gertrud accepted the strenuous factory work as a challenge, as an occasion for "learning" and for proving her own invulnerable inner strength: "I soon came to the point of seeing the factory work not simply as a harsh necessity, as coercion, but as a kind of lesson, and I wanted to learn as much as possible." [84]

> I was sitting in our locker room during the breakfast break (about fifteen minutes) alone on a bench together with a young gypsy woman who did nothing, said nothing, only looked out motionlessly onto the empty factory yard . . . I observed her; she didn't have the sharp gypsy face with the restless flashing eyes, her features were soft, rather Slavic, she was also comparatively light . . . And on her face lay not only this dullness, this yielding expression as in animals, in old draft horses—certainly that too, but more: an impenetrable aloofness, a silence, a distance, which could not be reached by any word or any look from the outside world . . . And I realized: That was what I always wanted to possess, though I never quite succeeded; for if I had it no one on the outside

would be able to touch me. But I am on my way to achieving this and it makes me glad . . .[85]

My acquaintance Dr. H. was a Spinoza scholar and spoke with me one day about the theory of the freedom of the human will amidst unfreedom. I told him that I understood this well from my own experience. Because I could not choose to accept or reject the factory work I was ordered to do; I had to give in and do it. But I *was* free to *inwardly* reject or accept it, to resist it or to approach it with good will. At the moment that I *accepted* it in my heart, there was no more pressure weighing on me; I was determined to see it as a lesson and to learn as much as possible. In this way I was free in the midst of my subjugation.[86]

While employed in Lichtenberg Gertrud Kolmar grew to love her fellow workers, especially those Jews from the lower classes whom she really came to know for the first time in her life. This new affinity became all the more evident to her when, in 1942, she was transfered to another factory in Charlottenburg, this time to work among women of her own social background: "('This woman is the nicest guy in the whole plant,' the worker U. in Lichtenberg, formerly a waiter, once said of me behind my back; here the opinions about me would probably be quite different.) At the same time, according to 'upbringing' I belong to the same social circles as my fellow workers here, whereas the men in L. usually came from a socially less fortunate class. And I got along with them, but not with these women. Perhaps because race is stronger than class, because the men, for better or worse, were Jews, and these ladies, in a bad, purely superficial sense, appeared assimilated, and could not see their way clear to being Jews after they had not been Jews for decades." [87]

But there was another kind of affection which Gertrud

found at the factory. Her letters describe with moving simplicity the story of her "romance" with a young medical student—he twenty-two, she forty-eight. Always a lover in her poetic work, it appears that Gertrud Kolmar remained so in life, presumably to the very end. The last mention of the young man, who obviously meant a great deal to her, occurs in a letter of February 20, 1943, just one week before her deportation.

Despite her courageous attempts to adapt to the regimentation of the factory, the long hours of work and commuting left her exhausted and unable to write for several months. But even these hardships could not long suppress her innate will to create. By March 5, 1942, she is able to report a new story,[88] conceived under even more discouraging circumstances than was *Susanna*:

> A few months ago I would not have considered it possible under such physical strain; but look, I've managed it! . . . Of course it is "only" prose, not verse; what I am writing is a story; in any case this ability to create again after a long pause is an unexpected gift. The little work is growing extremely slowly, but all the same it is growing, usually mornings while I am getting up and getting dressed, and during the subway trip; during the breakfast break I scrawl it down on a piece of paper. And when I have made even a little progress with it and feel that what I have done is good and beautiful, then at times I am very happy . . . Then I think it must be a real, genuine art which is not dependent on hours of leisure nor desk and chair, nor a quiet room, nor any exterior calm or comfort, but is able to conquer every adversity of time and space . . .

Indeed, the most memorable thing about the letters of Gertrud Kolmar is the evidence they give of her ability to conquer such adversity, and of her enormous heroism in the face of so much affliction: "The earlier decades when we were doing 'very well' were not for me, they demanded qualities of a gregarious, social kind that, for the most part, I lacked; but what the present demands—that I have in every way; I am a good match for today." [89] The basis of this remarkable fortitude lies in Gertrud's ability to transcend the very "present day reality" to which she proclaims herself equal. On August 4, 1942, she declares: "I am coming ever closer to the point of completely ridding myself of the nonessential, of inwardly removing myself from it." And on August 8 she describes her utter detachment from the outside world: "Yesterday in the subway it was so strange: as if all these talking, moving people were distant from me; because I was dead and far above them, above their petty affairs, above any association with them. Such peace was inside me then and such a deep, lasting silence . . ."

In September, 1942, Gertrud's father was deported to the extermination camp at Theresienstadt, probably under the pretense of being sent to an old people's home. Now it would be little more than five months before Gertrud herself, saved from earlier deportation by her status as a laborer, would face the end. Her last letter is dated the 20th and 21st of February, 1943. She must have been arrested, along with most other forced laborers in Berlin, on February 27. The camp to which she was deported was almost certainly Auschwitz. Her time of death is unknown.

There can be little doubt that she was fully prepared to die. As all her last letters indicate, Gertrud Kolmar was able to face all adversities and, one feels certain, her ultimate destruction as well, with perfect equanimity because she had developed an almost superhuman capacity to accept the inevitable. Like the Spartans and the Roman stoics she so admired, she possessed the wisdom of *amor fati*, love of fate. One of her last letters contains a moving affirmation of her faith in that wisdom, a statement that well could stand as her epitaph:

So I will step beneath my fate, be it high as a tower, be it black and oppressive as a cloud. Even though I do not know what it will be: I have accepted it in advance, I have given myself up to it, and know that it will not crush me, will not find me too small. How many of those who today break down at the very sight of a destiny too great for them have asked themselves whether they do not deserve some punishment, whether they must not atone for something? I was no worse than other women in my thoughts and deeds. But I knew I did not live the way I should have, and I was always ready to do penance. And all the grief that came over me and may come over me I will take upon myself as atonement, and it will be just. And I will bear it without complaining and somehow find that it belongs to me and that I was born and have grown to endure it and somehow to outlive it.[90]

HENRY A. SMITH

Charlottesville, Virginia
March, 1973

Image of Woman

Die Dichterin

Du hältst mich in den Händen ganz und gar.

Mein Herz wie eines kleinen Vogels schlägt
In deiner Faust. Der du dies liest, gib acht;
Denn sieh, du blätterst einen Menschen um.
Doch ist es dir aus Pappe nur gemacht,

Aus Druckpapier und Leim, so bleibt es stumm
Und trifft dich nicht mit seinem großen Blick,
Der aus den schwarzen Zeichen suchend schaut,
Und ist ein Ding und hat ein Dinggeschick.

Und ward verschleiert doch gleich einer Braut,
Und ward geschmückt, daß du es lieben magst,
Und bittet schüchtern, daß du deinen Sinn
Aus Gleichmut und Gewöhnung einmal jagst,

Und bebt und weiß und flüstert vor sich hin:
»Dies wird nicht sein.« Und nickt dir lächelnd zu.
Wer sollte hoffen, wenn nicht eine Frau?
Ihr ganzes Treiben ist ein einzig: »Du . . .«

Mit schwarzen Blumen, mit gemalter Brau,
Mit Silberketten, Seiden, blaubesternt.
Sie wußte manches Schönere als Kind
Und hat das schönre andre Wort verlernt. –

The Woman Poet

You hold me now completely in your hands.

My heart beats like a frightened little bird's
Against your palm. Take heed! You do not think
A person lives within the page you thumb.
To you this book is paper, cloth, and ink,

Some binding thread and glue, and thus is dumb,
And cannot touch you (though the gaze be great
That seeks you from the printed marks inside),
And is an object with an object's fate.

And yet it has been veiled like a bride,
Adorned with gems, made ready to be loved,
Who asks you bashfully to change your mind,
To wake yourself, and feel, and to be moved.

But still she trembles, whispering to the wind:
"This shall not be." And smiles as if she knew.
Yet she must hope. A woman always tries,
Her very life is but a single "You . . ."

With her black flowers and her painted eyes,
With silver chains and silks of spangled blue.
She knew more beauty when a child and free,
But now forgets the better words she knew.

Der Mann ist soviel klüger, als wir sind.
In seinem Reden unterhält er sich
Mit Tod und Frühling, Eisenwerk und Zeit;
Ich sage: »Du . . .« und immer: »Du und ich.«

Und dieses Buch ist eines Mädchens Kleid,
Das reich und rot sein mag und ärmlich fahl,
Und immer unter liebem Finger nur
Zerknittern dulden will, Befleckung, Mal.

So steh ich, weisend, was mir widerfuhr;
Denn harte Lauge hat es wohl gebleicht,
Doch keine hat es gänzlich ausgespült.
So ruf ich dich. Mein Ruf ist dünn und leicht.

Du hörst, was spricht. Vernimmst du auch, was fühlt?

A man is so much cleverer than we,
Conversing with himself of truth and lie,
Of death and spring and iron-work and time.
But I say "you" and always "you and I."

This book is but a girl's dress in rhyme,
Which can be rich and red, or poor and pale,
Which may be wrinkled, but with gentle hands,
And only may be torn by loving nails.

So then, to tell my story, here I stand.
The dress's tint, though bleached in bitter lye,
Has not all washed away. It still is real.
I call then with a thin, ethereal cry.

You hear me speak. But do you hear me feel?

Die Unerschlossene

Auch ich bin ein Weltteil.
Ich habe nie erreichte Berge, Buschland undurchdrungen,
Teichbucht, Stromdelta, salzleckende Küstenzungen,
Höhle, drin riesiges Kriechtier dunkelgrün funkt,
Binnenmeer, das mit apfelsingelber Qualle prunkt.

Meiner Brüste Knospen spülte nicht Regen,
Kein Strahl riß sie auf: diese Gärten sind abgelegen.
Kein Abenteurer hat noch meiner Wüstentäler goldenen
    Sand besiegt
Und den Schnee, der auf hohen Öden jungfräulich liegt.

Nacktrote Felsgurgel würgen Kondore mit kralligen Fingern,
Spreiten die Federmäntel in Lüfte und ahnen nichts von
    Bezwingern.
Sind Adler? Auch Urweltadler – wer lauschte, wenn einer
    schrie? –
Doch meine großen Geier sind mächtiger noch und fremder
    als sie.

Was ich hülle, bricht nie mehr aus schon erschlossenen Erden;
Denn dort leitet kein Schlangenwidder starr zuckende
    Vipernherden,
Leuchten durch Nächte nicht Kröten sich mit dem Karneol
    im Haupt.
Der Geheimnisse kupferner Kelch ward längst aus dem
    wehrenden Moos geklaubt.

Über mir sind oft Himmel mit schwarzen Gestirnen, bunten
    Gewittern,

Woman Undiscovered

I too am a continent.
I have unexplored mountains, bushlands impenetrable and lost,
Bays, stream-deltas, salt-licking tongues of coast,
Caves where giant crawling beasts gleam dusky green,
And inland seas where lemon-yellow jellyfish are seen.

No rains have washed my budded breasts,
No springs burst forth from them: these gardens are remote from all the rest.
And no adventurer has claimed my desert valley's golden sands,
Or crossed the virgin snows atop my highest barren lands.

With taloned fingers condors strangle naked gullets of red stone,
Spread feathered coats in air, suspect no master, and abide alone.
Are eagles there, primordial? And who would hear if one would scream?
But my great vultures are more powerful than they, and stranger than a dream.

What I conceal will never break from cultivated soil;
For there no serpent rams lead herds of snakes that twitch and coil,
No toads shine through the night with reddish gems imbedded in their heads.
The copper chalice long ago was dug from clinging moss; its secrets are all dead.

Above me, often skies are black with stars or bright with thunderstorms;

In mir sind lappige, zackige Krater, die von zwingendem
Glühen zittern;
Aber auch ein eisreiner Quell und die Glockenblume ist da,
die ihn trinkt:
Ich bin ein Kontinent, der eines Tages stumm im Meere
versinkt.

Inside me flicker lobed and jagged craters filled with violent
glowing forms;
But an ice-pure fountain I have as well, and the flower that
drinks there quietly:
I am a continent that one day soon will sink without a
sound into the sea.

Troglodytin

Und ich muß durch Dunkelheiten
Wie durch große Wälder spähn,
Selbst die Schrecken mir bereiten,
Die sich meinen Stapfen blähn,
Brandgestruppte Elche, Bachen,
Grunzend um das Ferkelblut,
Wölfe, hungergrau, und Drachen
Mit den Waben gelber Glut.

Nackt, auf scharf bekrallten Zehen,
Rot von Schauern ausgewetzt,
Im Geröhr an Sumpf und Seen
Duck ich brünstig und gehetzt;
Natter schlüpft durch meine Hände,
Schnecke näßt mein Haar mit Schleim,
Meine buntgefärbte Lende
Wird der Kröte liebes Heim.

Meine Zähne reißen Beulen
Von verkrustet hartem Stamm;
Ein beglücktes, leises Heulen,
Brech ich hoch aus Ried und Schlamm,
Eh der Leib mit Bärenpranken
Um den irren Wandrer ringt,
Ihn, erglüht, an Brust und Flanken
Keuchend sich zu Willen zwingt.

Auf verdorrten schwarzen Kräutern
Lieg ich stumm im Höhlenhaus;
Schwer an trankgeschwellten Eutern

Troglodyte

Through the darkness I must peer
As if through great forest lairs.
Even creatures cause me fear,
Prowling in my steps: the bears,
Shaggy elks, the wild boars
Grunting over piglet's blood,
Hungry wolves, and dinosaurs
Gleaming ochre in the mud.

Nude, I crouch on taloned toes
Sharpened red on rended meat;
In the reeds of swampy groves
I hide hunted and in heat.
Vipers wriggle through my fingers,
Snails wet my hair with slime,
And around my loins there linger
Colored toads of many kinds.

Tearing teeth crack brittle bones,
Crusted stems and hardened seeds.
Suddenly, with howling moans
Out I leap from mud and weeds,
Claws and body dragging down
A wanderer who lost his way.
Breast and flanks force to the ground . . .
Gasping, I devour my prey.

My cave house is black as ink;
There I lie on dried leaf mats,
And on udders swelled with drink

Hängen Kind und Fledermaus,
Da im Mondforst Auerhähne
Eine Hexe bellend neckt,
Die mit fahler Widdermähne
Goldne Kringelhörner deckt.

Heavy hang a child, a bat.
Outside in the moonwood howls
A witch and frights the unicorn.
On her head a ram's-wool cowl
Covers golden curving horns.

Mädchen

Ich will in meinem Bette ruhn und die Erde bedecken.
Über den Ländern Europas und Afrikas liege ich da.
Meinen linken Arm will ich tief hinein nach Asien strecken.
Und den rechts nach Amerika.
Mein schlängelndes Haar wird im Nordmeer den Alk
erschrecken.

Zischende Augen will in das weiche Dunkel ich bohren
Wie farbigen Stahl, der die kühle Haut verglüht und
zerreißt,
Mit meiner Nacktheit leuchten dem, der die Straße verloren,
Der meine Stätte ungewiß suchend umkreist,
Und mich mit Schweigen verkleiden vor brüllenden Kehlen,
versiegelten Ohren.

Mein bleiches Kissen: Eisberg, den Nacht umflutet.
Ich schmelze ihn hin mit dem Tropenstrauß meiner Hand,
Mit Irisblüten, golden und braunrot durchblutet;
Graubläuliche Otter hält sie leicht wie ein Band,
Flüstert Wunder mir zu, die sie weiß und vermutet.

Und ein Wunder ist dies: es spritzen feurige Funken
Aus der Glut. Den Himmel brennt Mondnarbe, Sternenmal.
Und der Erde gereiftes Brot wird verteilt, ihr Wein wird
getrunken.
Wasser scheint immer noch zart und wallend und fahl,
Hegt den stummen mächtigen Hai und das Läuten
gelbbauchiger Unken.

Girl

I will rest on my bed and cover the earth.
Over the lands of Europe and Africa I lie,
My left arm reaching deep into Asia,
And the right towards America.
My snaking hair will frighten the auk in Arctic seas.

My hissing eyes into the down of darkness bore
Like molten steel that rends and sears cool skin;
My nakedness will light a path for him who lost his way
And circles searchingly around my resting place;
And I will clothe myself in silence against strident voices
    and deafened ears.

My pale pillow is an iceberg buoyed by night.
It melts away beneath my tropic hands
That bloom like iris blossoms, veined with golden blood;
They hold the gray-blue ribbon of an adder
Who whispers to me wonders that he knows.

And this too is a wonder: fiery sparks that spray
And burn the heavens with a lunar scar and starry wounds.
The ripened bread of earth is shared, and wine is poured.
With pale waves the waters still shine soft
That hold the mute and mighty shark and the croaking of
    gold-bellied toads.

Düster und Strahl sind um mich. So sind sie gewesen,
Da der Ägypter den Königen steinerne Gräber getürmt,
Noch die Sibylle ihre verkohlten Bücher gelesen,
Da erzürnte Harpyien das Mahl des Phineus umstürmt.
Da Juda die Götzenhäuser gefegt mit glänzendem Besen.

Nun verbergen Menschen die Bläue mit speienden Schloten,
Fürchten das Erdgespenst nicht mehr, den klagenden Wolf,
Schirren die Luft und fahren in steigenden Booten
Über Woge und Welt, spielen Tennis und Golf
Und schlafen dann hundert Jahre unter den Toten.

Wie der Sand, wie Flamme und Fluten, so unabwendlich,
Wie Wolke, so unentrinnbar bin ich.
Einst ziehen Kindesgeschlechter, fern mir und nicht mehr
verständlich,
Horizonthin, versunkenen Sonnensterns bluthellen Strich.
Mein Tag hat sein Maß, doch meine Nacht ist unendlich.

O Männer. Ihr mögt mit Maschinen rasen, tausend
elektrische Lampen entzünden,
Ihr schwächt nicht die Faust, die euch zu mir reißt.
Mein Weiher und tiefes Lächeln liegt zwischen dämmrigen
Schlünden,
Erwartet still euren neuesten, schwächlich geblähten,
unbeständigen Geist
Und wirft eine Welle aus seinem Schoß; sie schluckt ihn
samt seinen Gründen.

Kommt ihr mit tanzenden Tieren, mit dem Scherenschleifrad
zur Stadt, seid Bürger, seid Grafen,
Füße laufen wie schneeweiße Ratten euch nach,
Laufen immer: Füße kupferhaariger Nächte im Hafen,

The gloom and light surround me as they were
When kings of Egypt towered stony tombs,
As when the sibyls read their charcoal books,
And angry harpies stormed the feast of Phineas,
Or when great Judah swept the shrines with shining brooms.

But now men hide the sky with spewing smoke,
And fear no more the ghosts, the wailing wolf.
They harness air and ride in climbing boats
Across the world's waves, play cards and golf,
Then sleep a hundred years among the dead.

Like the sand, like flame and flood, as certain
As the clouds, I am eternal.
One day a child's crusade will pass me far away, its meaning lost,
In pilgrimage toward the sunken sun-star's blood-bright band.
My daytime has its measure, but my night remains unending.

Oh men, though you may rush in cars and light electric lamps,
You will not stop my hands that draw you near.
My pool, my smile, set still amid unfathomable gulfs
Awaits the next brief swelling of your fragile thought,
And swallows it in waves poured from its womb.

And though you come to town with dancing bears, a scissors-grinder or a prince,
My feet will follow you like snow white rats,
Will follow always: feet of bronze-haired nights in harbors,

Wenn euer Schiff die grüne schaumkrallige Pranke zerbrach,
Sie lassen euch unter dem Südlichen Kreuz, dem Großen
Wagen nicht einsam schlafen.

Die Liebkosung eurer Lippen, Gier eurer Hände
Sammle ich ein, und die Freude, die aus euren Augen
schlägt,
In ein seidenes Vogelgarn, das ich trage an meiner Lende,
Wie das Känguruh seinen Beutel trägt.
Und ich füge die glühenden Stunden und finstere zu
funkelnder Spende.

Goldflossige Fische schwimmen, lautlose Kiemen, in Bütten,
Die meine weiten Abende sind.
Und der Kometenregen will alles dies achtlos verschütten
Über ein Kind.
Es ist zart und ewig und nur wie die bräunlichen Kleinen
schindelgedeckter Hütten.

When your ship was crushed in claws of greenish waves;
They'll never let you sleep alone beneath the Dipper or the Southern Cross.

Caresses from your lips, lust from your hands
And pleasures from your eyes I catch
Within a silken snare worn at my loins,
A soft marsupial pouch,
And blend the glowing hours and dark into a shining gift.

Fish swim, gold-finned, with soundless gills in wooden troughs
That are the broad expanses of my evenings.
And still the rains of comets thunder down and, heedless,
Drown a child:
Eternal, fragile, like the brownish babes in shingle-covered huts.

Du

Du. Ich will dich in den Wassern wecken!
Du. Ich will dich aus den Sternen schweißen!
Du. Ich will dich von dem Irdnen lecken,
Eine Hündin! Dich aus Früchten beißen,
Eine Wilde! Du. Ich will so vieles –
Liebes. Liebstes. Kannst du dich nicht spenden?
Nicht am Ende des Levkojenstieles
Deine weiße Blüte zu mir wenden?

Sieh, ich ging so oft auf harten Wegen,
Auf verpflastert harten, bösen Straßen;
Ich verdarb, verblich an Glut und Regen,
Schluchzend, stammelnd: ». . . über alle Maßen . . .«
Und die Pauke und das Blasrohr lärmten,
Und ich kam mit einer goldnen Kette,
Tanzte unter Lichtern, die mich wärmten,
Schönen Lichtern auf der Schädelstätte.

Und ich mochte wohl in Gärten sitzen,
Auch den Wein wohl trinken aus der Kelter,
Doch die Lider klafften, trübe Ritzen,
Und ich ward in Augenblicken älter.
Und auf meinen Leichnam hingekrochen
Ist die Schnecke träger Arbeitstage,
Zog den Schleimpfad dünner grauer Wochen,
Schlaffer Freude und geringer Plage.

In den Wäldern bin ich umgetrieben.
Ich verriet den Vögeln deinen Namen,
Doch die Vögel sind mir ferngeblieben;

You

You. I want to wake you in the waters!
You. I want to melt you from the stars!
You. I want to lick you from the earth,
A bitch! And bite you out of fruit,
A savage! You. I want so much—
Dear. Dearest. Can't you give yourself to me?
And spend the blossoms, white,
Atop your flowering stem?

For I have often trudged along hard paths,
On paved, hard roads and over evil streets;
I languished, weathered by the glare and rain,
And, sobbing, stammered: ". . . more than I can
  stand . . ."
The kettle drum and brasses toned aloud;
And then I entered wearing golden chains,
And danced beneath the lights that gave me warmth,
The lovely lights upon the place of skulls.

And well I would desire to sit in gardens,
Well would drink the new wine from the press;
But eyelids yawned and shut to gloomy slits,
And I became in fleeting moments older.
Upon my corpse the snail has crawled,
The snail of sluggish working days
That trailed a thin gray path of weeks,
Of feeble joys and meager discontent.

In woods I wandered near and far,
And told the birds your name,
Yet I remained a stranger to the birds;

Wenn ich weinte, zirpte keiner: Amen.
Und die Scheckenkühe an den Rainen
Grasten fort mit seltnem Häupterheben.
Da entfloh ich wieder zu den Steinen,
Die mir dieses Kind, mein Kind nicht geben.

Einmal muß ich noch im Finstren kauern
Und das Göttliche zu mir versammeln,
Es beschwören durch getünchte Mauern,
Seinem Ausgang meine Tür verrammeln,
Bis zum bunten Morgen mit ihm ringen.
Ach, es wird den Segen nimmer sprechen,
Nur mit seinem Schlag der erznen Schwingen
Diese flehnde Stirn in Stücke brechen. . .

For when I wept not one would sing amen.
The dappled cows that ranged along the ridge
Continued grazing, seldom raised their heads.
So off I ran, returning to the stones
Which cannot give the child that I desire.

And now once more I cower in the dark,
Collecting godliness about me,
And call it forth through blank white walls,
And barricade my door to keep it in.
Then I will wrestle with it 'til the dawn.
But, oh, it never will pronounce its blessing!
Will only strike me with its brazen wings
And break my supplicating brow in pieces!

Die Sünderin

Wem sollte ich meine rote Hölle schenken?
Wem meinen malvenfarbenen Himmel zwischen Abend
    und Nacht
Mit Lampen, dickflüssig gelb aus Eidotter gemacht,
Und der sich auf die Stadt hinlegt, lastend wie Denken?

Dieser Stadt Häuser haben seltene Türme.
Ihre Dächer steigen, Gebirg, in die freien Lüfte ein;
Sie heißen Gesetz und Sitte, manche auch Anstand und
    Schein.
Ummauerte Gäßchen, häßliche Namen, verkriechen sich
    wie Gewürme.

Mir ward all das Kriechende längst von goldenen Flammen
    zerrissen;
Nicht stand ich in heimlichen Toren, gierig, lachte dem Dieb,
Zuckte glänzende Schultern aus Fetzen, lüstern: Hast
    du mich lieb?
Ich trug die ewig glühende Kohlenkrone, trug sie auf
    meinem Gewissen.

Einmal ward sie entzündet, verschlungen, gesteigert
In unendliches Wehn, feuerwipfligen Wald.
Ihre Zunge schlug in den Mund, der meinen Schenkel
    umkrallt,
Und nie hat sich stürzender Funke den starken, den reinen
    Händen des Jünglings geweigert.

Er hielt ihn hinauf in Nacht als schmerzende Leuchte,
Und hält er ihn durch sein Leben als unaufhörlichen Brand,

The Sinner

Whom should I give my flame-red hell?
Whom my mauve-toned sky between the dusk and dark,
With lamps like egg-yolks, flowing molten gold,
A sky that weighs upon the town like heavy thought?

This town has houses with strange, towering roofs
That rise like mountains in the open air;
They're called the law or custom or propriety or show.
Walled alleyways with ugly names creep off to hide like worms.

For me these crawling things have long been swallowed up by golden flames.
I never stood in secret doorways, greedy, laughing to the thieves,
Nor lifted shining shoulders out of rags to sell my love.
I wore upon my conscience the eternal glowing crown of coals.

One day it was ignited and engulfed in flames,
And grew to endless waves, a forest with its treetops all ablaze.
Its tongue drove down the mouth that grasped my thigh,
And never did a single spark refuse a lover's strong pure hands.

He held it high into the night, a painful torch,
And kept it through his life, a ceaseless flame.

So wird es geklärt, erscheinend und eingeschmolzen dem
Land,
Das keine erstickenden Moore schleppt voll laulicher
Feuchte.

Das ist wahr. Ich bin nicht die Lasterhafte. Ich bin nicht
die Böse,
Die dem Toten die Mannheit raubt, des Vogels kindliches
Auge durchsticht,
Die dem vertrauenden Knaben den zarten Wirbel zerbricht.
Ich fresse mich selbst in dem sengenden Schrei: Erlöse!

Jenen, die auf dem Holzstoß prasselnde Bisse zermalmen,
Bin ich gleich, ich, das Weib, das Geschlecht, Mutter,
Gebärerin.
Über die Zeugenden, die Gezeugten lodert mein Herz ewig
hin.
Meine Seele kniet und singt Psalmen.

Thus it was purified and shines and melts into a land
That bears no suffocating marshes full of tepid slime.

All that is true. I am not sinful, am not evil,
Do not steal the manhood of the dead or stab the childlike
eyes of birds,
Or break the trusting infant's tender spine.
I gnaw myself away in burning cries: oh set me free!

I am as martyrs burning at the stake, devoured by snapping
fangs
A woman, mate and mother, pregnant womb.
Above all those who now beget and are begotten blazes my
eternal heart.
And yet my soul kneels down and chants the psalms.

Verwandlungen

Ich will die Nacht um mich ziehn als ein warmes Tuch
Mit ihrem weißen Stern, mit ihrem grauen Fluch,
Mit ihrem wehenden Zipfel, der die Tagkrähen scheucht,
Mit ihren Nebelfransen, von einsamen Teichen feucht.

Ich hing im Gebälke starr als eine Fledermaus,
Ich lasse mich fallen in Luft und fahre nun aus.
Mann, ich träumte dein Blut, ich beiße dich wund,
Kralle mich in dein Haar und sauge an deinem Mund.

Über den stumpfen Türmen sind Himmelswipfel schwarz.
Aus ihren kahlen Stämmen sickert gläsernes Harz
Zu unsichtbaren Kelchen wie Oportowein.
In meinen braunen Augen bleibt der Widerschein.

Mit meinen goldbraunen Augen will ich fangen gehn,
Fangen den Fisch in Gräben, die zwischen Häusern stehn,
Fangen den Fisch der Meere: und Meer ist ein weiter Platz
Mit zerknickten Masten, versunkenem Silberschatz.

Die schweren Schiffsglocken läuten aus dem Algenwald.
Unter den Schiffsfiguren starrt eine Kindergestalt,
In Händen die Limone und an der Stirn ein Licht.
Zwischen uns fahren die Wasser; ich behalte dich nicht.

Hinter erfrorener Scheibe glühn Lampen bunt und heiß,
Tauchen blanke Löffel in Schalen, buntes Eis;
Ich locke mit roten Früchten, draus meine Lippen gemacht,
Und bin eine kleine Speise in einem Becher von Nacht.

Metamorphoses

I will draw the night around me like a warm shawl
With its one white star, its grayish pall,
Its windblown corners scattering the crows of day,
Its foggy fringes dipped in waters far away.

A bat, I hang down rigid from a rafter,
Drop free and catch your scent and follow after.
Oh, man, I dream your blood; my bite is death.
I'll claw into your hair and suck your breath.

On tower stumps rise heaven's black treetops.
From barren branches glassy resin drops
In unseen goblets like Oporto wine.
Within my brown eyes dark reflections shine.

With my gold-brown eyes I'll catch my prey,
Catch the fish in ditches dug in clay,
Catch the fish at sea; and the sea is wide and old,
With broken masts and sunken chests of gold.

The heavy bells of ships ring out in seaweed groves.
Among the figureheads a child's figure moves,
A lemon in its hands, a light within its brow.
Between us flow the waters; I'll never hold you now.

Behind frozen panes the bright, hot lamps entice,
And shiny spoons dip sherbet's colored ice.
I lure with reddish fruits: I offer lips to bite;
And am a tiny morsel in a dish of night.

Meerwunder

Als ich das Kind mit grünen Augensternen,
Dein zartes, wunderbares Kind empfing,
Erbrausten salzge Wasser in Zisternen,
Elmsfeuer funkelten aus Hoflaternen,
Und Nacht trug den Korallenring.

Und deiner Brust entwehte Algenmähne
So grün, so grün mit stummer Melodie.
Sehr sachte Fluten plätscherten um Kähne,
Im schwarzen Traumschilf sangen große Schwäne,
Und nur wir beide hörten sie.

Du warst den Meeren mitternachts entstiegen
Mit eisig blankem, triefend kühlem Leib.
Und Wellenwiegen sprach zu Wellenwiegen
Von unserm sanften Beieinanderliegen,
Von deinen Armen um ein Weib.

Seejungfern hoben ungeschaute Tänze,
Und wilde Harfen tönten dunkel her,
Und Mond vergoß sein silbernes Geglänze
Um den Perlmutterglast der Schuppenschwänze;
Mein Linnen duftete vom Meer.

Und wieder wachten Hirten bei den Schafen
Wie einst . . . und glomm ein niebenannter Stern.
Und Schiffe, die an fremder Küste schlafen,
Erbebten leis und träumten von dem Hafen
Der Heimat, die nun klein und fern.

Sea-Monster

When I conceived the child with star-green eyes,
Conceived your child, this frail and wondrous thing,
We heard salt water in the cisterns sigh,
Saw Elmo's fire in lanterns 'gainst the sky,
And midnight wore its coral ring.

And from your breast a seaweed mane was flowing,
So green, so green, with silent melody.
And quiet ripples splashed from gentle rowing,
From black dream-rushes songs of swans were blowing,
And no one else could hear but we.

At midnight you had risen from the sea,
Your body dripping cool and icy smooth.
The ocean spoke a hushed soliloquy
Of how you lay so gently next to me
And how your arms embraced and soothed.

Sea-virgins came and swam mysterious dances;
Dark music from wild harps resounded free.
The moon poured out its light in silvery lances
On pearly scales and submarine romances;
And all my sheets smelled of the sea.

And once again the shepherds watched their flocks,
And, as before, there shone an unnamed star.
And ships that lay at anchor by strange rocks
Tossed in their sleep and dreamed of distant docks,
The ports of home, now small and far.

Tierblumen waren fächelnd aufgebrochen,
In meinen Schoß verstreut von deiner Hand;
Um meine Füße zuckte Adlerrochen,
Und Kinkhorn und Olivenschnecke krochen
Auf meiner Hüfte weißen Sand.

Und deine blaß-beryllnen Augen scheuchten
Gekrönte Nattern heim in Felsenschacht,
Doch Lachse sprangen schimmernder im Feuchten;
An Wogenkämmen sprühte blaues Leuchten
Wie aus dem Rabenhaar der Nacht.

O du! . . . Nur du! . . . Ich spülte deine Glieder
Und warb und klang und schäumte über dir.
Und alle Winde küßten meine Lider,
Und alle Wälder stürzten in mich nieder,
Und alle Ströme mündeten in mir.

And fans of flower-beasts broke open wide,
Spread out across my body by your hand,
While manta-rays swam round me with the tide
And olive-snails and periwinkles plied
Across my dune-white hip of sand.

The glances of your pale beryl eyes
Chased hooded vipers home to caves in flight,
While shining salmon leapt toward the skies.
Bright beads of spray on wave-tops crystallized,
Blue as the raven hair of night.

Oh you! Your body sank into my sea;
I wooed and sang and swept you like a shoal.
And all the winds blew kisses and caressed me.
And all the forests toppled down within me.
And all the rivers ran into my soul.

Eine Mutter

Du Liebes.
Meine Arme halten dich
Wie einen Blumenkorb.
Ein Frühlingseiland: weiße Hyazinthen,
Blaukrokus, honigfarbne Märzenbecher,
Der seltnen Tulpe lilagraue Tinten.
Und deine Knospenaugen fallen auf wie Fächer
Und schaun in mich.

Was siehst du da? Nur dich.
Und wieder dich.

Mein Kind.
Ich rühre dich mit Mund und Nüstern an
Wie schönes Obst auf einer Schale.
Da Herb und Süß sich neidlos mengt:
An Pflaumen, dunkelhäutige Ovale,
Sich würzig derbes Nußvolk purzelnd drängt,
Der Saftzitrone jüngferliche Fahle
Ein Traubenzweig mit glühnden Tropfen sprengt –

So rühre ich dich an.
Mein Kindlein!
Bist du, was ich sagen kann?

O Muschel, zartes Rauschen.
Freude. Sternenbild.
Ach, alle Namen werden schal vor dir.
Ich schließe dich im Herzen ein
Wie einen Becher, den ich nicht zu nützen wage,
Aus Onyxstein.

A Mother

Oh dearest one!
My arms embrace you
Like a basket of flowers.
Springtime island: snow-white hyacinths,
A deep blue crocus, honey-colored narcissus,
The gray and lilac hues of rarest tulips.
And your floral eyes fall open like a fan
And look at me.

What do you see? Yourself.
Only yourself.

My child.
I touch you with my mouth and nostrils
Like a lovely fruit inside a bowl
Where sweet and bitter mingle naturally:
On dark skinned oval plums
Press clustered hard and aromatic nuts.
The juicy lemon's virgin flush
Rests by a grape vine with its glowing drops.

And so I touch you.
Precious child!
Can you be anything I say?

Oh seashell, gentle rushing.
Happiness. Sky full of stars.
Oh child, all names are meaningless compared to you.
I close you in my heart
Like some rare chalice made of onyx stone
I dare not use.

Wie eine wunderbare Sage
Vom kupfernen und grünen Tier.
Und eine kleine Waffe wider dürre Tage.
Du Rosenquarz. Du Licht!

Ich spreche irr. Mein Dunkel ruft dich mir.
In meinem Tage bist du nicht.

Or like a wondrous legend
Of a great green copper beast.
A tiny weapon against barren days.
You, my rose-quartz. Oh my light!

My words are mad. My darkness calls you to me.
For in all my days you never were.

Spielzeug

Der kleine Seehund ist ein Spiel im Kasten,
In hohler Brust die Schraube.
Er träumt ein Schiff mit Himmel an den Masten
Und weißer Segelhaube.

Er schaut den glasgegoßnen Schaum der Kronen,
Darüber Möwen singen,
Die Beete, bunt mit Meeresanemonen
Und Quallenschmetterlingen.

Ihr Kinder, laßt ihn kreisen um die Tische,
Ihn fahren an den Wänden,
Und reicht ihm frische Nahrung, Zauberfische,
In euren jungen Händen.

Die Wellen steigen mit kristallnen Spitzen,
Umklingen eure Säume,
Tangbärte kriechen grün aus Dielenritzen
Und rot Korallenbäume.

Südwestwärts tanzen kleine blaue Stühle
Die munterste Quadrille;
Sie schmecken fernen Duft durch Salz und Kühle
Von Zimmet und Vanille.

In eurer Bettstatt aber lagert Norden
Mit Schnee in kahlen Schluchten.
Der Eisbär springt von flutzerrißnen Borden,
Und wilde Vögel wuchten.

Toy

The little seal's a plaything made of brass,
His flippers hold a screw.
He dreams a ship with sky above its mast
And sails all white and new.

He watches foamy waves, like beaded glass,
And hears the seagulls' cries,
Sees colored beds of ocean flowers and grass,
And sunfish butterflies.

You children, let him circle round the dishes
And cross the table lands,
And give him food to eat, some magic fishes,
Out of your little hands.

The waves surge up and down with crystal points,
And rush around your knees.
Green seaweed beards grow out of table-joints,
And orange coral trees.

Southwestwards now the little yellow chairs
Are dancing a quadrille;
They sniff a distant smell on salt-cool airs
Of cinnamon-vanilla.

But on your bed lie winter's arctic snows
With ice and bare crevasses.
The polar bear leaps over crumbling floes,
And wild birds fly in masses.

An bloßen Füßen saugt die Spindelschnecke,
Spielt Drachenkopf und Rochen;
Hoch über euch ist platte Mörteldecke
Zur Wolke aufgebrochen,

Die groß sich vor dem Abendblick gestaltet,
Ein Traum und eine Dolde,
Und jede graue Blume still entfaltet
Aus einem Kelch von Golde.

Around your naked toes suck little snails,
And starfish swim in crowds.
High overhead the plaster ceiling sails
All broken up with clouds,

Which now before your drowsy evening eyes
Into a dream unfold,
And every still gray flower multiplies
Out of a cup of gold.

Schlaf

Dein weicher Mund liegt saugend an den Sphinxbrüsten
meines Throns.
Mir zieht sein Durst herauf, und ich geb ihm zu trinken.
Ich bin der Schlaf. Ich rühr ihn mit Blättern blauen Mohns,
Die leicht wie Fächer auseinandersinken.

Sie sind bedeckt mit schwarzen Schattenrissen,
Die Farb und Leben ihm zeigen, der sie gen Mitternacht hält,
Wenn groß dein junger Atem hinrollt über die Kissen
Und deinem Arm das kleine pelzige Spieltier entfällt.

Denn gar nichts Wirkliches zieht mit dir durch die Pforte ein,
Wenn du kommst, meine schöne Laterna magica anzusehn.
Du weißt: Die erste war Gold, die zweite war Erz, die dritte
war Elfenbein –
Und nur durch die Elfenbeintür darfst du straflos gehn.

Wir haben orangenes Licht, wenn das lila erlosch:
Da schreitet die Königin mit dem Eidechsenschwanz,
Da reitet der dicke Bauer auf einem gelbbäuchigen Frosch
Und sattelt die arme Magd ihre schneeweiße Gans.

Die feuerbemalte Trommel brummt in das Schellenhüpfen.
Ihr letztes Dröhnen schüttelt das Ei des Vogels Rock.
Du siehst ein seltsames Junges der krachenden Schale
entschlüpfen
Mit Löwenklau, mit Adlerflug und Hörnern gleich dem Bock.

Die Hörner sprießen lang, durchbohren den Stern
Und spalten sich, zackig zerklüftet, Zähne von Riesen.

Sleep

Your gentle mouth lies nursing at the sphynx-breasts of
    my throne.
Your thirst has drawn you to me, and I give you drink.
For I am sleep. I brush you now with opium's blue tone,
With leaves that fan apart and gently sink.

And they are filled with darkened silhouettes
That show, when held toward midnight, colored forms,
When your young breath rolls vast across the coverlets,
And toy fur animals escape your arms.

For nothing real can follow through the gates at dusk
When you arrive to see my magic lantern glow.
You see: the first was gold, the second bronze, the third
    was tusk,
And through the ivory gate alone it's safe to come and go.

And we have orange lights when purple lights go out,
To watch the queen parading with her lizard's tail,
Observe fat farmers riding frogs with yellow snouts,
And see the goose-girl on her snowbird sail.

The fire-painted drum resounds among the jingling bells.
Its last roll rattles eggs inside the nest of giant rocs.
You see the strange young birds emerging from their broken
    shells,
With lion's claws and eagle's wings and horns of giant
    bucks.

The horns sprout long and bore into a star,
And split, all cleft and jagged, into titans' teeth.

Irgendwo sank ein Tal, ganz tief und ganz fern,
Mit stillen Birnbaumgärten und Pustblumenwiesen.

Zwischen den weißen Sonnen geht deine Mutter spazieren.
Hinter ihr wandeln ein Rind und ein Dromedar.
Sie trennt sich deutlich und klein von den fließenden Tieren.
Vielleicht sind es Träume – aber vielleicht ist es wahr.

Somewhere a sinking valley founders deep and far
With quiet pear-tree orchards and a dandelion heath.

Between the gleaming suns your mother walks.
Behind her stroll a cow, a kangaroo.
So small, she stands apart from shapeless beasts that stalk.
Perhaps these all are dreams, perhaps all true.

Mörder

Die Mörder gehen in der Welt herum.
Die ganze Nacht, o Gott, die ganze Nacht!
Sie suchen dieses Kind, das in mir angefacht
So wie ein Licht, erscheinend, mild und stumm.

Sie wollen es doch löschen. Wie ein Schattenquellen
Entrinnen sie aus winkligem Gebäu,
Wie magre Katzen, die sich scheu
Hinducken über ausgetretne Schwellen.

Und ich bin an mein Bett geschweißt
Mit dürrer Kette, die der Rost zerfrißt
Und die doch schwer und gänzlich ohne Mitleid ist,
Nur eiternde Geschwulst aus meinen Armen beißt.

Der Mörder kommt ja schon. Er trägt den Hut,
Einen breiten Hut mit Turmkopf, ungeheuer;
Am Kinn sproßt kleines gelbes Feuer.
Es tanzt auf meinem Leib; es ist sehr gut . . .

Die große Nase schnüffelt, längert sich
Zu dünnem Rüssel. Wie ein Faden.
Aus seinen Fingernägeln kriechen Maden
Wie Safran, fallen auch auf mich.

In Haar und Augen. Und der Rüssel tastet
Auf meine Brüste, nach den rosabraunen Warzen.
Ich seh ihn weißlich fleischlich winden sich im Schwarzen,
Und etwas sinkt an mich und keucht und lastet —

Murder

The murderers are loose! They search the world
All through the night, oh God, all through the night!
To find the fire kindled in me now,
This child so like a light, so still and mild.

They want to put it out. Like pouring ink
Their shadows seep from angled walls;
Like scrawny cats they scuttle
Timidly across the footworn steps.

And I am shackled to my bed
With grating chains all gnawed with rust
That weigh upon me, pitiless and strong,
And bite raw wounds into my helpless arms.

The murderer has come! He wears a hat,
A broad-brimmed hat with towering pointed peak;
Upon his chin sprout tiny golden flames
That dance across my body; it is good . . .

His huge nose sniffs about and stretches out
Into a tentacle that wriggles like a rope.
Out of his fingernails crawl yellow maggots,
Saffron seeds that sprinkle down on me

Into my hair and eyes. The tentacle
Gropes for my breasts, at rose-brown nipples,
And I see its white flesh twist into the blackness;
Something sinks upon me, sighs and presses—

Ich kann nicht mehr . . . ich kann nicht . . . Laß die
Schneide schlagen
Als einen Zahn, der aus dem Himmel blitzt!
Zerstoße mich! Da wo der Tropfen spritzt:
Hörst du ihn »Liebe Mutter« sagen?

Hörst du —? O still. In meinem Schoße ruht das Beil.
Von seinen Seiten brechen eibenhaft zwei Flammen;
Sie grüßen sich und falten sich zusammen:
Mein Kind. Aus dunkelgrüner Bronze, ernst und steil.

I can't go on . . . I can't . . . Oh let the blade strike down
Like a monstrous tooth that flashes from the sky!
Oh crush me! There, where blood-drops fly,
Can you hear it cry, can you hear it?

"Mother!" Oh the stillness . . . In my womb: the axe.
From either side of it break forks of flame.
They meet and fold together now:
My child. Of dark green bronze, so stern and grave.

Komm

O komm.
Du amethystenes Gewölbe großer Nacht.
O komm.
Du goldgestickte Decke über süßen Broten.
O komm.
Sternsamen, aus dem himmlischen Getreide rieselnd sacht.
O komm.
Du kupferdunkle Schlange, die mit Lebensgeifer spritzt die
Toten.

O komm.
Du überm Alltag schwebende, verzückte Melodie,
O komm.
Ich möchte einmal dich mit Lippen fassen, eh ich sterbe.
O komm.
Du meine braune Rose. Solche gab es nie.
O komm.
Du samtner Taumund voll unsäglich süßer Herbe.

O komm.
Grau riesenhafter Turm, der in die Öden floh.
O komm.
Ich duck mit Schleierkäuzen mich am Fenster ohne Scheibe.
O komm.
Du steinernes Gesetz, das bröckelnd stürzte irgendwo.
O komm.
Ich richte die geborstne Tafel auf an finstrer Eibe.

O komm.
Du Zauberspange, die der unverstandne Spruch durchflicht.

Come

Oh come.
Thou vault of amethyst, enormous night.
Oh come.
Thou gold-embroidered cloth on fragrant bread.
Oh come.
Thou granary of stars with sifting seeds of light.
Oh come.
Thou serpent, copper dark, who sprays life's venom in the dead.

Oh come.
Ecstatic melody that soars above the everyday,
Oh come.
I want to seize you with my lips before I die.
Oh come.
My red-brown rose so rare and far away.
Oh come.
Thou velvet mouth of dew so filled with spices sweet and dry.

Oh come.
Gray, monumental tower that fled into the barren night.
Oh come.
I crouch with barn-owls on a broken window's sill.
Oh come.
Thou stony law that crumbling sank from sight.
Oh come.
And I will raise the shattered tablet on some somber hill.

Oh come.
Thou magic ring, round-woven with mysterious signs.

O komm.
Mein Haupt in Ruhe, meine Stirn in Schlaf zu schließen.
O komm.
Du blauer Brunnen, der aus jeder Blume eine schöne Iris
bricht.
O komm.
Du Regenbogenweinen, grasgesäumtes Fließen.

O komm.
Mein Kind. O komm, o komm, du Kind.
O komm.
Mein hohler Paukenschlag kann mich nicht mehr betäuben.
O komm.
Und willst du nicht, so nimm mich in den Wind.
O komm.
Und laß mich überm Meere, Ockersand, verstäuben.

Oh come.
And close my head in quietness, my brow in sleep.
Oh come.
Blue-rushing spring that breaks an iris out of every vine.
Oh come.
Thou weeping rainbow, fringed with grass and flowing deep.

Oh come.
My child. Oh come, oh come, my child.
Oh come.
My hollow drumbeat deadens me no more.
Oh come.
And if you will not come, then take me in a tempest blowing wild.
Oh come.
And cast my dust upon a distant shore.

Winter

Der Triefbart zackt vereist vom Regenrohr.
Nordost steift wölfisch das gespitzte Ohr.

Ein Stern friert bläulich an, von Dunst umdickt.
Der Neuschnee klingelt glasbehängt und tickt.

Und Krähen schwimmen in den Acker schwer,
Der starre Wellen schlägt, ein schweigend Meer.

Ich steh am Uferwege, welk und klein,
Und senkte gern der Schäumeflut mich ein,

Die Fischernetze toter Amseln schleppt,
In steinern grünlich dunklen Abend ebbt.

Leicht splittert von der Wunde meiner Brust,
Dem schwarzen Kreis, ein Vogel ab: Gekrust.

Der Schneeglanz spült ihn hin: verdorrter Klang,
Der Regenbogen über Wälder sang.

Ich blieb. Durch meine Lider stichelt Reif.
Und hinterm Auge, weit, zerfließt ein Streif

In Grau und Rosa. Blaß verwischter Steig.
Ein Silberkelch, aprilner Pfirsichzweig,

Der leise, dichte Bienensüße weht.
Die Woge atmet in ein Scillabeet

Den stummen Fittich aus: er dehnt sich matt . . .
Kalt bleicht die Mondstirn, die kein Antlitz hat.

Winter

An icy beard stabs jagged from the drain.
The Northeast stiffens wolfish pointed ears.

A blue star freezes fast in thickened fumes.
The new snow jingles glass-bedecked and ticks.

And swarms of crows swim heavy in the field
Becalmed with rigid waves, a silent sea.

I stand along the shoreline, limp and small,
And wish to sink into the drifting flood

Whose fishnets drag dead blackbirds in their ebb
Toward the dark green stone of growing night.

A splinter from the crusted wound I hide,
A bird breaks off to join the dusky crowd.

The snow-sheen sweeps him off: a withered cry
The rainbow sang above the frozen woods.

I stayed. And hoarfrost pricks into my lids.
Behind my eyes, far distant, fades a stripe

To gray and rose. Pale disappearing path.
A silver bloom, an April peachtree branch,

That gently blows a bee-sweet, thick perfume.
The wave breathes out into a flower bed

Its silent wings: it widens languidly . . .
Cold pale, the moon-disc stares without a face.

Die Jüdin

Ich bin fremd.

Weil sich die Menschen nicht zu mir wagen,
Will ich mit Türmen gegürtet sein,
Die steile, steingraue Mützen tragen
In Wolken hinein.

Ihr findet den erzenen Schlüssel nicht
Der dumpfen Treppe. Sie rollt sich nach oben,
Wie platten, schuppigen Kopf erhoben
Eine Otter ins Licht.

Ach, diese Mauer morscht schon wie Felsen,
Den tausendjähriger Strom bespült;
Die Vögel mit rohen, faltigen Hälsen
Hocken, in Höhlen verwühlt.

In den Gewölben rieselnder Sand,
Kauernde Echsen mit sprenkligen Brüsten —
Ich möcht eine Forscherreise rüsten
In mein eigenes uraltes Land.

Ich kann das begrabene Ur der Chaldäer
Vielleicht entdecken noch irgendwo,
Den Götzen Dagon, das Zelt der Hebräer,
Die Posaune von Jericho.

Die jene höhnischen Wände zerblies,
Schwärzt sich in Tiefen, verwüstet, verbogen;
Einst hab ich dennoch den Atem gesogen,
Der ihre Töne stieß.

The Jewish Woman

I am a stranger.

Since no one dares approach me
I would be girded with towers
That wear their steep and stone-gray caps
Aloft in clouds.

The brazen key you will not find
That locks the musty stair. It spirals skyward
As a serpent lifts its scaly head
Into the light.

Oh these walls decay like cliffs
That streams have washed a thousand years;
And birds with raw and wrinkled craws
Lie burrowed deep in caves.

Inside the halls of sifting sand
Crouch lizards hiding speckled breasts—
An expedition I would mount
Into my ancient land.

Perhaps somewhere I can unearth
The buried Ur of the Chaldeans,
The idol Dagon, Hebrew tents,
Or the horn of Jericho.

What once blew down the haughty walls
Now lies in twisted ruin underground;
And yet I once drew breath
To sound its note.

Und in Truhen, verschüttet vom Staube,
Liegen die edlen Gewänder tot,
Sterbender Glanz aus dem Flügel der Taube
Und das Stumpfe des Behemoth.

Ich kleide mich staunend. Wohl bin ich klein,
Fern ihren prunkvoll mächtigen Zeiten,
Doch um mich starren die schimmernden Breiten
Wie Schutz, und ich wachse ein.

Nun seh ich mich seltsam und kann mich nicht kennen,
Da ich vor Rom, vor Karthago schon war,
Da jäh in mir die Altäre entbrennen
Der Richterin und ihrer Schar.

Von dem verborgenen Goldgefäß
Läuft durch mein Blut ein schmerzliches Gleißen,
Und ein Lied will mit Namen mich heißen,
Die mir wieder gemäß.

Himmel rufen aus farbigen Zeichen.
Zugeschlossen ist euer Gesicht:
Die mit dem Wüstenfuchs scheu mich umstreichen,
Schauen es nicht.

Riesig zerstürzende Windsäulen wehn,
Grün wie Nephrit, rot wie Korallen,
Über die Türme. Gott läßt sie verfallen
Und noch Jahrtausende stehn.

Inside chests choked with dust
Lie dead the noble robes,
The dying gleam of pigeons' wings,
And the torpor of Behemoth.

Amazed, I clothe myself. For I am small
And far from ages glorious and strong.
Yet all about me stare expanses shining:
Shelter for my soul.

Now I seem strange, no longer know myself,
For I was there before great Rome and Carthage were,
Because in me the altar fires ignite
Of Deborah and her tribe.

And from the hidden golden bowl
A painful glistening runs into my blood,
And then a song rings out a name
That suits me once again.

The heavens call with colored signs.
Your face is closed:
And those who steal around me with the desert fox
Will never see it.

Enormous, crumbling columns of wind,
As green as nephrite, red as coral,
Blow across the towers. God lets them fall in ruin,
And yet they stand for ages more.

Wir Juden

Nur Nacht hört zu. Ich liebe dich, ich liebe dich, mein Volk,
Und will dich ganz mit Armen umschlingen heiß und fest,
So wie ein Weib den Gatten, der am Pranger steht, am Kolk
Die Mutter den geschmähten Sohn nicht einsam sinken läßt.

Und wenn ein Knebel dir im Mund den blutenden Schrei
verhält,
Wenn deine zitternden Arme nun grausam eingeschnürt,
So laß mich Ruf, der in den Schacht der Ewigkeiten fällt,
Die Hand mich sein, die aufgereckt an Gottes hohen Himmel
rührt.

Denn der Grieche schlug aus Berggestein seine weißen
Götter hervor,
Und Rom warf über die Erde einen ehernen Schild,
Mongolische Horden wirbelten aus Asiens Tiefen empor,
Und die Kaiser in Aachen schauten ein südwärts gaukelndes
Bild.

Und Deutschland trägt und Frankreich trägt ein Buch und
ein blitzendes Schwert,
Und England wandelt auf Meeresschiffen bläulich silbernen
Pfad,
Und Rußland ward riesiger Schatten mit der Flamme auf
seinem Herd,
Und wir, wir sind geworden durch den Galgen und durch
das Rad.

We Jews

The night alone can hear. I love you, I love you, oh my people,
In my embrace I want to hold you warm and close
Just as a wife would hold her husband on the scaffold steps,
Or like a mother who cannot allow her son to die alone.

And when your throat is gagged, your bleeding cry suppressed,
When brutal shackles bind your trembling arms,
Oh let me be the voice that echoes down the shaft of all eternity,
The hand stretched high to touch God's towering heaven.

For the Greeks have struck white gods like sparks from mountain crags,
And Rome threw brazen shields across the earth,
Mongolian hordes whirled forth from deep in Asia,
And the emperors in Aachen gazed enchanted to the South.

And Germany and France hold high their books and shining swords,
And England wanders silver paths on ocean-going ships,
And Russia grew to giant shadows with a flame upon its hearth,
And we, we have proceeded through the gallows and the rack.

Dies Herzzerspringen, der Todesschweiß, ein tränenloser
Blick
Und der ewige Seufzer am Marterpfahl, den heulender
Wind verschlang,
Und die dürre Kralle, die elende Faust, die aus Scheiter-
haufen und Strick
Ihre Adern grün wie Vipernbrut dem Würger entgegenrang,

Der greise Bart, in Höllen versengt, von Teufelsgriff zerfetzt,
Verstümmelt Ohr, zerrissene Brau und dunkelnder Augen
Fliehn:
Ihr! Wenn die bittere Stunde reift, so will ich aufstehn hier
und jetzt,
So will ich wie ihr Triumphtor sein, durch das die Qualen
ziehn!

Ich will den Arm nicht küssen, den ein strotzendes Zepter
schwellt,
Nicht das erzene Knie, den tönernen Fuß des Abgotts
harter Zeit;
O könnt ich wie lodernde Fackel in die finstere Wüste der
Welt
Meine Stimme heben: Gerechtigkeit! Gerechtigkeit!
Gerechtigkeit!

Knöchel. Ihr schleppt doch Ketten, und gefangen klirrt mein
Gehn.
Lippen. Ihr seid versiegelt, in glühendes Wachs gesperrt.
Seele. In Käfiggittern einer Schwalbe flatterndes Flehn.
Und ich fühle die Faust, die das weinende Haupt auf den
Aschenhügel mir zerrt.

This bursting of our hearts, this sweat of death, this gaze without a tear,
And the eternal windblown sigh of martyrs at the stake,
The withered claw, the weary fist with veins like vipers
Raised against the murderers from ropes and funeral pyres of ages,

The gray beard singed in hellfires, torn by devils-grip,
The mutilated ear, the wounded brow and fleeing eye:
Oh all of you! Now, when the bitter hour strikes I will arise
And stand like a triumphal arch above your cavalcade of anguish!

I will not kiss the arm that wields the weighty scepter,
Nor the brazen knee, the earthen feet of demigods in desperate hours;
If only I could raise my voice to be a blazing torch
Amidst the darkened desert of the world, and thunder: JUSTICE! JUSTICE! JUSTICE!

And yet my ankles are in chains; I drag a ringing prison as I go.
My lips are sealed in glowing wax.
My soul is like a swallow fluttering helpless in its cage.
And I can feel the fist that drags my weeping head toward the hill of ashes.

Nur Nacht hört zu. Ich liebe dich, mein Volk im Plunderkleid.
Wie der heidnischen Erde, Gäas Sohn entkräftet zur Mutter
glitt,
So wirf dich du dem Niederen hin, sei schwach, umarme das
Leid,
Bis einst dein müder Wanderschuh auf den Nacken der
Starken tritt!

The night alone can hear. I love you, oh my people dressed
in rags.
Now, like the son of Gaea who returned exhausted to his
heathen mother earth,
So you must cast yourselves among the lowly and be weak;
embrace your sorrow.
For one day your weary wandering shoes will stand upon
the necks of all the mighty!

Die Sinnende

Wenn ich tot bin, wird mein Name schweben
Ein kleine Weile ob der Welt.
Wenn ich tot bin, mag es mich noch geben
Irgendwo an Zäunen hinterm Feld.
Doch ich werde bald verlorengehn,
Wie das Wasser fließt aus narbigem Krug,
Wie geheim verwirkte Gabe der Feen
Und ein Wölkchen Rauch am rasenden Zug.

Wenn ich tot bin, sinken Herz und Lende,
Weicht, was mich gehalten und bewegt,
Und allein die offnen, stillen Hände
Sind, ein Fremdes, neben mich gelegt.
Und um meine Stirn wirds sein
Wie vor Tag, wenn ein Höhlenmund Sterne fängt
Und aus des Lichtgewölbs Schattenstein
Graues Tuch die riesigen Falten hängt.

Wenn ich sterbe, will ich einmal rasten,
Mein Gesicht nach innen drehn
Und es schließen wie den Bilderkasten,
Wenn das Kind zuviel gesehn,
Und dann schlafen gut und dicht,
Da ich zittrig noch hingestellt,
Was ich war: ein wächsernes Licht
Für das Wachen zur zweiten Welt.

Meditation

When I am dead my name will glide
Above the world a little while.
When I am dead I might still hide
Somewhere beyond the field, across the stile.
But I will soon be lost and gone,
Drained from a broken basin like the rain,
Like a secret gift the fairies have withdrawn,
Or a puff of smoke from a speeding train.

When I am dead my heart and breast
Will fade. What moved, what strengthened me will change
To nothing, and my hands alone will rest
Beside me: quiet, open, strange.
Above my forehead, as before the end of night,
A cavern's mouth will swallow all the stars,
And, hung from shadow-stone in vaulted light,
A huge, gray drapery will fold enormous bars.

When I must die, I want to stop and rest,
And turn my face inside,
And close it like a picture-chest
In which a child has looked and cried.
Then deep and well I'll sleep the night,
For I have left a thing for which I stand:
A trembling waxen light
To watch until I wake into another land.

Die Begrabene

Wir folgten alle einem Ziel,
Und was uns hielt, war Lust und Spiel,
Und was uns trieb, war Sorg und Not,
Und was uns lohnte, war der Tod.

Nun lieg ich friedlich hingestreckt
Und bin mit Erde zugedeckt;
»Ich brauch und habe« blieb nicht mein,
»Ich muß und werde« ließ mich sein.

Im Lichtland ist Verwesung froh;
Sie färbt ihr Kleid mit Indigo,
Trägts heute glatt und morgen kraus
Und baut den Turm von Babel aus.

Sie hetzt ihr Bild auf Leinewand,
Sie pfählts an Zaun und Zeitungsstand,
Ihr leeres Gieren grinst und rafft
Und heißt Erfolg und Wissenschaft.

Mit rohem Wahnwerk, grassem Mord
Zerschlägt sie hundertsten Rekord,
Im Sarge tobt sie durch die Welt –
Wann findet sie das Gräberfeld?

Sie siegt im Schrei, im Sprung, im Lauf;
Da wacht die Grube endlich auf,
Hat einmal gähnend sich gereckt
Und sie mit Erde zugedeckt.

The Buried Woman

In life we all pursued our aims.
What held us up was lust and games.
What drove us on was want and strife,
And what we earned: an end to life.

So now I lie stretched out alone,
All covered up with earth and stone.
"I have and want" I cannot say;
"I must and will" became my way.

In lands of light exults decay.
He clothes himself as blue as day;
In many forms deceives the eye,
And builds the tower of Babel high.

We see his face in movie halls
And nailed to newsstands, fences, walls;
His name is there for all to see;
"Success," he's called, "Technology."

His cruel machines, his brutal crimes
Break every record of our times.
His coffin governs East and West.
But will it soon be laid to rest?

The victory of death seems near.
But no! At last a grave appears,
Awakens, yawns its jaws to bite,
And crushes death in lasting night.

Abschied

Nach Osten send ich mein Gesicht:
Ich will es von mir tun.
Es soll dort drüben sein im Licht,
Ein wenig auszuruhn
Von meinem Blick auf diese Welt,
Von meinem Blick auf mich,
Die plumpe Mauer Täglich Geld,
Das Treibrad Sputedich.

Sie trägt, die Welt in Rot und Grau
Durch Jammerschutt und Qualm
Die Auserwählten, Tropfentau
An einem Weizenhalm.
Ein glitzernd rascher Lebenslauf,
Ein Schütteln großer Hand:
Die einen fraß der Mittag auf,
Die andern schluckt der Sand.

Drum werd ich fröhlich sein und still,
Wenn ich mein Soll getan;
In tausend kleinen Wassern will
Ich rinnen mit dem Schwan,
Der ohne Rede noch Getön
Und ohne Denken wohl
Ein Tier, das stumm, ein Tier, das schön,
Kein Geist und kein Symbol.

Und wenn ich dann nur leiser Schlag
An blasse Küsten bin,
So roll ich frühen Wintertag,

Farewell

Into the East I send my face:
I'm giving it away.
And in some distant sunlit place
A moment it should stay
And rest from gazing out at life,
From watching all my ways,
From vulgar haste and gold and strife:
The mill-wheel "everyday."

The world goes on through waste and pain,
Through smoke, through red and gray.
The chosen ones, a drop of rain
Upon a stalk of hay.
A bright career, complete so soon.
A shaking of distinguished hands:
And one is swallowed by the noon,
Another lost in sands.

Thus cheerful I'll remain, and still,
When life has come and gone.
Into a thousand streams I'll spill
And swim beside the swan,
Who, without speech and without tone,
Perhaps without a mind,
Remains a lovely beast alone,
No intellect, no sign.

And finally, when I fade away,
A wave on pale coasts,
I'll wash to sea a winter's day,

Den silbern kühlen Sarkophag
Des ewigen Todes hin,
Darin mein Antlitz dünn und leicht
Wie Spinneweben steht,
Ein wenig um die Winkel streicht,
Ein wenig flattert, lächelnd bleicht
Und ohne Qual verweht.

A sepulcher of frigid gray,
Death's everlasting ghost.
Inside, my fragile face will stay
As I sail round the bend,
And I will smile and drift away,
And disappear in wind and spray
To meet a painless end.

Animal Dreams

Die Reiher

Die schwarzen Reiher flogen über grüngoldnes Birken-
gerinnsel:
Pfeilvögel, Speervögel mit starren Schnäbeln und Stelzen,
An einen rosa Himmel getuscht von chinesischem Pinsel
Unter Gewölkburgen, die in rauchblauen Ost sich wälzen.

Der Vögel verwunderte Augen spiegeln gewichtlose Erze,
Abends Geglüh. Sie zielen in reglose Ferne mit Hälsen.
Fort, fort über Hutweidenpappel, einsam auflodernde
Kerze,
Fort, über Wildsuhle fort, umbäumt von finsteren Elsen.

Sie kennen nicht Fall aus der Höhe, nicht Beutelockung,
Ermatten.
Ihre Gefährten schlürften aus Teich, dem bauchigen Kruge,
Duckten sich dann ins Wipfelnest: Wärme und Schatten;
Ihnen sickern Gestirne milchig und kalt aus dem Fluge.

Warf eine starke Hand sie auf schwebende Reise,
Um von Nachtwelt mit ewigen Flügeln den Lichtstaub
zu wischen
Oder am Ausgang des Alls doch nur bekömmliche Speise,
Sättigungslust aus trübem Tümpel zu fischen?

Die Reiher flogen ... Kleiner als eine Motte,
Nur scharf und dunkel der erste, den Spähblick einfangen
konnte;
Der zwölfte schien heller und größer. Ein Letzter der Flotte
War dunstig grau und bedeckte die Horizonte.

The Herons

Black herons flew over green-golden masses of birch trees,
Soaring like javelins, spear-birds with bills and legs rigid,
Inked with a Chinese brush onto a rose-colored sky
Under great castles of cloud that roll eastward to smoke-
blue horizons.

Wondering eyes of the birds mirror weightless hot metals—
Evening's glow. Their necks aim into motionless distance.
Way and away over poplars like lone glowing candles,
Onward they fly over waterholes bounded by dark alder
trees,

Knowing no fall from the heavens, nor lure, nor exhaustion.
Others have sipped from the pond, from the potbellied
pitcher,
Slipped into tree-crowning nests full of warmth and dark
shadows;
Flying they stream out behind them the milk of the cold
constellations.

Could a strong hand have propelled them aloft on their
voyage,
To sweep with perpetual wings the light's dust from the
night-world,
Or, seeking felicitous food on a far-dismal shoreline,
To fish for the lust of fulfillment in ponds at the ends of the
earth?

The herons flew onward . . . Though small as a moth now,
But black, sharply outlined, the leader was still within sight.
The twelfth bird seemed brighter and larger. The last of the
fleet
Was gray as a fog and enormous, his wings covering both
the horizons.

Trauerspiel

Der Tiger schreitet seine Tagereise
Viel Meilen fort.
Zuweilen gegen Abend nimmt er Speise
Am fremden Ort.

Die Eisenstäbe: alles, was dahinter
Vergeht und säumt,
Ist Schrei und Stich und frostig fahler Winter
Und nur geträumt.

Er gleitet heim: und mußte längst verlernen,
Wie Heimat sprach.
Der Käfig stutzt und wittert sein Entfernen
Und hetzt ihm nach.

Er flackert heller aus dem blinden Schmerze,
Den er nicht nennt,
Nur eine goldne rußgestreifte Kerze,
Die glitzernd sich zu Tode brennt.

Tragedy

The tiger walks his daily beat
Of many paces.
Sometimes at dusk he takes his meat
At foreign places.

Beyond the iron bars, things far away
That move and gleam
Are noises from a faded winter day
And like a dream.

He slinks toward home, but no more can recall
The jungle's way.
Surprised, the cage now senses his withdrawal
And traps its prey.

He smoulders with a blind and senseless dread
He cannot name.
A candle striped with soot and golden red,
He burns himself to death in sparkling flame.

Die Kröte

Ein blaues Dämmer sinkt mit triefender Feuchte;
Es schleppt einen breiten rosiggoldenen Saum.
Schwarz steilt eine Pappel auf in das weiche Geleuchte,
Und milde Birken verzittern zu fahlerem Schaum.
Wie Totenhaupt kollert so dumpf ein Apfel zur Furche,
Und knisternd verflackert mählich das herbstbraune
Blatt.
Mit Lichtchen gespenstert ferne die düsternde Stadt.
Weißer Wiesennebel braut Lurche.

Ich bin die Kröte.
Und ich liebe die Gestirne der Nacht.
Abends hohe Röte
Schwelt in purpurne Teiche, kaum entfacht.
Unter der Regentonne
Morschen Brettern hock ich duckig und dick;
Auf das Verenden der Sonne
Lauert mein schmerzlicher Mondenblick.

Ich bin die Kröte.
Und ich liebe das Gewisper der Nacht.
Eine feine Flöte
Ist im schwebenden Schilf, in den Seggen erwacht,
Eine zarte Geige
Flirrt und fiedelt am Felderrain.
Ich horch und schweige,
Zerr mich an fingrigem Bein

Unter fauler Planke
Aus Morastigem Glied um Glied,

The Toad

The bluish twilight sinks with dripping dews,
Dragging behind its broad, rose-golden fringes.
Lone poplars stand out black on soft pale hues;
A tender birch dissolves to mist-gray tinges,
And apples roll like skulls toward the furrows.
The leaves, like crackling embers, fade to brown,
While ghostly lamps peer from a distant town.
White meadow fog brews beasts within their burrows.

I am the toad.
I love the stars of night.
The coals of sunset, evening's ruddy lode,
Smoulder in purple ponds, barely alight.
Beneath the rainbarrel's sodden wood
I crouch, low, fat, and wise.
My painful moon-eyes wait and brood
To view the sun's demise.

I am the toad,
And whispering night is my abode.
A slender flutist stirs
And sings in swaying reeds and sedge.
A velvet violinist whirrs
And fiddles at the field's edge.
I listen, silent, from my soggy seat.
Then, pushing with my fingery feet,

Beneath the rotten planks I creep.
Out of the morass, inch by inch I wind,

Wie versunkner Gedanke
Aus dem Wust, aus dem Schlamm sich zieht.
Durch Gekräut, um Kiesel
Hüpf ich als dunkler, bescheidener Sinn;
Tauiges Laubgeriesel,
Schwarzgrüner Efeu spült mich dahin.

Ich atme, schwimme
In einer tiefen, beruhigten Pracht,
Demütige Stimme
Unter dem Vogelgefieder der Nacht.
Komm denn und töte!
Mag ich nur ekles Geziefer dir sein:
Ich bin die Kröte
Und trage den Edelstein...

Like a thought that, buried deep,
Emerges from a muddled mind.
Through weeds I hop and over gravel,
A dark and humble sense.
Over dew-soaked leaves I travel
Toward the black-green ivy by the fence.

I breathe and swim
Upon a peaceful deep.
And from the garden's rim,
With modest voice I peep
Amid the feathered night, and rest
Defenseless. So be cruel—
Come kill me! Though to you I'm but a pest:
I am the toad, and wear a precious jewel . . .

Der Geier

Du hältst die Flügel gebreitet
Über ein Lehen von Licht.
Die Zeit, die kränkend schreitet,
Welkt deine Blume nicht:
Blume, fleischroter Lappen,
Flockfeder, schwarz oder rein;
Hakige Fänge schnappen
Den runden Erdklumpen ein.

Du zwingst mit ihrem Griffe
Die Welten, neu und alt,
Südsee-Korallenriffe
Und den brasilianischen Wald.
Du stürzest in ihrem Griffe
Die Welten, neu und alt,
Eismeers krachende Schiffe
Und die Höhle von Basalt.

Deine Schwingspitzen rosten
Am himmlischen Erzdach fest;
Die eine haftet im Osten,
Die andere zeigt nach West.
Dein kahler Schrei springt in Stürme;
Der einsam Erkennende siecht,
Wenn Wintermond, totes Gewürme,
Dem Schnabel maisgelb entkriecht.

Wie meutrisch Vulkane flammen,
Kalt funkelnde Gletscher zertaun,
Du krallst den Brocken zusammen,

The Vulture

You hold your wings outspread,
Lord over leagues of light.
Time rudely strides ahead,
But cannot reach or blight
Your flower, the flesh-red craw,
Or feathers black and gray.
Your clutching talons claw
The earth: a lump of clay.

They master East and West,
The New World and the Old,
And seize the Andes' crest
And South-Sea reefs of gold.
You snatch into their grip
The New World and the Old,
The Arctic's cracking ships
And caverns' granite cold.

Rusted to the iron tent
Of sky, your wingtips rest,
One fixed in the Orient,
The other pointing west.
Your stark voice sings in squalls;
And watching, man lies ill
When winter's moon-worm crawls
Corn-yellow from your bill.

As mad volcanoes spurt,
Cold-sparkling glaciers slide,
You clench the clods of dirt

Drin Ameisenstädte sich baun,
Und senkt sich loderndste Mähne
Im Schauen deines Gesichts,
Es fällt keine einzige Träne
Dir fern in unendliches Nichts.

Where anthill cities hide.
And when your blazing head
Looks down upon our earth,
No single tear is shed
Into the endless dearth.

Hyänen

Wie die Sterne heulen, o, wie die Sterne heulen!
Wie sie greulich lachen und murren und ächzen!
Wie sie niederhüpfen von zwölfmal hohen Säulen,
Weil sie nach dem Aas der blutigen Erde lechzen!

Sie sind herabgekommen, sie sind eingeschlichen
In der Hunde Leiber, tückische Sterndämonen;
An ihrer Bosheit ist der glänzende Pelz verblichen,
Doch auf den Spitzohren tanzen blaue Flämmchenkronen.

Wie die Teufel klagen, o, wie die Wüsten klagen!
Ihr giftiges Funkelauge, Gier in ihren Zähnen!
Wie sie plündernd und schändend über Leichen lagen
Mit grauenhaftem Gekicher, in Wollust, Hyänen!

Geht nicht hinaus, ihr Männer, haltet euch stille, Knaben,
Daß sie euch nicht opfern auf ihren Höllaltären
Und ihr einst, entmannt, wenn Monde gewandelt haben,
Brüste der Weiber schleppt und könnet doch nie gebären.

Laßt die Teufel sich balgen um zernagten Knochen,
Über Eselsgerippen häßlich geifern und höhnen!
Morgen sind sie wieder in Nachtgestirne verkrochen,
Wenn eure Herzen preisen, wenn eure Lippen tönen.

Manchmal scheinen sie tot mit versteinten Augen,
Die ein Zauberer sucht, schneidet zu Latwergen,
In roten Mörsern stampft, löst in ätzenden Laugen —
Doch wenn der Fromme sich naht, soll er sein Antlitz
bergen!

Hyenas

How the stars are howling, oh, how the stars are howling!
How horribly they laugh and snarl and groan!
How they jump down from their mile-high pillars growling,
Hungry for the carrion of bloody earth and stone!

They have come down, they have climbed
Into the bodies of dogs. Astral demons, sly and untamed;
Their evil pales the gleaming fur they find,
And on their pointed ears dance blue tufts of flame.

How the devils cry, oh how the deserts cry!
Poison in their sparkling eyes, greed in their fangs!
How they plunder and rape! Over corpses they lie
Laughing madly with lust, the hyena gangs!

Oh men, don't venture out! Boys, stay inside!
Or on their hellish altars you may learn to grieve,
And then, emasculated, when a new moon rides
You drag a woman's breasts, but cannot conceive.

Let the devils grab at bones and claw and fight,
Let them slaver on a skeleton's decay.
Tomorrow they return to constellations of the night,
If only hearts will praise and lips will pray.

Sometimes they seem dead, with stony eyes
That a sorcerer seeks and kneads like clay,
Grinds in mortars, dissolves in burning lyes—
But if a good man meet them, let him look away!

Der große Alk

Das war die Trauminsel, eine Schale voll Schnee,
Und riesiger Molchkamm, stand der Bergkette Eis;
Das war eine grünkristallne gefrorene See
Und drüber verwölkter Glasglocke milchiges Weiß.

Es stieg ein hoher Schrei und stob über Meer,
Und als unendlicher Stab floh sein Hall ihm nach;
Er aber selbst war die Spitze, der blitzende Speer,
So fuhr er in Frost, der klirrend erbebte und brach.

Und um meine Stirn schlug harschen Flugwindes Wehn
Und riß mich hin über gläsernen Rachen und Grat,
Das letzte Tier, das Tier vom Polarkreis zu sehn,
Das groß und rein aus der Menschenlosigkeit trat.

Es schien am Himmel, so ragte es über dem Meer,
Und konnte sprechen; aber es gab kein Wort.
Verkrüppelte Arme, hingen die Flügel ihm leer,
Und eine unendliche Einsamkeit stieß von ihm fort.

Es starrte aus Welt, dahin kein Taubengruß reicht,
Kein kreischender Sittichmund, kein rüttelnder Falk;
Ach, meine buntere Erde dünkte mir läppisch und seicht,
Und in diese wärmere Erde her horchte der Alk.

Da sprangen Schüsse, da klatschte blutender Fall,
Da wurden Mütter zerfetzt und Nester geraubt,
Und wieder: ein langes Wimmern schwankte ins All.
Der einsame Vogel warf das tropfende Haupt.

The Great Auk

There is an isle of dreams, a basin filled with snows,
And like a giant lizard's crest stand mountain chains of
brass;
There is a frozen sea of green and crystal floes,
And overhead a cloudy bell of milk-white glass.

A high-pitched cry shoots out across the sea,
And like an endless shaft, pursuing echoes flash;
He is the spearpoint then, and flying free,
He bores through rigid frosts that crack and crash.

Around my brow the raging, harsh winds fight
And sweep me over snowy jaws and broken glassy sheets
To see the farthest animal, the Arctic's anchorite
Emerging great and pure from uninhabited retreats.

He shines against the sky and towers over frozen tides,
And he can speak, but utters not a word.
Like crippled arms his wings hang empty at his sides
And endless solitude shines all about the lonesome bird.

He stares out from a world where no dove will alight,
No raucous parakeet will fly, nor darting hawk.
Oh now my brighter earth grows false and slight;
And, listening toward this warmer world, now waits the
auk.

And then there come the shots, the smack of a bloody fall;
Then nests are robbed, torn mothers left for dead.
Again: in endless space there reels a mournful call,
And silently the lone bird shakes his bleeding head.

Mörder Taube

O Krug, o Hafen, wer nur stürzte euch um?
Ich kehrte mich zu euch in einer jungen Nacht
Und spürte die fernen Hände, lieblich und stumm,
Die Wein aus Himmeln, Erde zu Brot gemacht.

Ich trank und aß und erblickte den roten Strom,
Der zart in mir glomm – als wär ich ein gläsernes Ding –
Und feines Goldstaubkorn mit süßem Arom,
Das durch mein Leben wie durch eine Sanduhr ging.

Und in meiner Mitte, da waren Ufer, war Land,
Da saß es wie Zwergenkind: Wesen, wunderlich klein;
Es grub seine Füße spielend in glitzernden Sand
Und tauchte den Finger sacht in die roten Quellbäche ein.

Ich wollte es küssen und rührte die Haut von Glas,
Die konnte ich nicht zerbrechen, weil selbst ich sie war;
Nun häufte sich Düne, und auf der Düne trieb Gras,
Wuchs hoch und dicht und grau und wucherte in mein Haar.

Es kam eine Taube, rosa und blaugrau, geschwebt
An einem bleichen Himmel. Der Himmel war nackt.
Ihr Schnabel schien mächtig, krumm und vom Blute verklebt
Der schwachen Gefährtin, der sie die Stirne zerhackt.

Und ich sah, wie es wirklich war, das lächelnde Perlglanzkleid,
Ich fand in ihm das Bild von den Tauben der Welt
Und fand aller Tauben Gier und Jähzorn und Neid.
So schwang sich der große Vogel über mein Feld.

Killer Dove

Oh urn, oh port, how were you overturned?
In early hours of night I looked for you,
And sensed the distant hands, lovely and still,
That made from heaven wine and bread from earth.

I drank and ate and saw the scarlet rills
That thinly shone, as if I were of glass,
And tiny grains of fragrant-smelling gold
Were sifted through my hourglass of life.

And deep inside me there were shores and land.
A fairy child, miraculous and small,
Was pushing playful feet in sparkling sand,
And dipped its finger in the ruddy streams.

I sought to kiss it, touched the glassy flesh,
But could not break it, for it was myself;
Then sand-dunes massed, and on them flourished grass
So tall and thick it twined into my hair.

There came a soaring dove, rose-blue and gray,
Emerging from a faded, naked sky.
His bill seemed mighty, curved and smeared with blood
Fresh stabbed out of his frail murdered mate.

I saw the truth inside the pearly cloak,
And saw in him the image of all doves,
The greed of doves, their jealousy and rage.
And then the giant bird lunged toward my land.

Und wo der Halm das verborgene Kind umstrich,
Da zückte er lang sanft schimmernder Schwingen Schlag,
Da sank er nieder, anmutig und fürchterlich,
Und es verging ein Blick und es verging ein Tag.

Und es verging ein Jahr. Und ich hob mich auf,
Ich rieb meine Augen, ich wußte kaum, was geschehn,
Erspähte die Inseln, suchte der Flüsse Lauf,
Das Kind, die Taube und konnte nichts mehr verstehn.

And where the grass caressed the hidden child
He drew the bright blade of his wingbeat's blow
And plunged sublime and terrible to earth.
And then a moment passed, and then a day.

A year passed by. And I awoke and rose
And rubbed my eyes, unsure of what had been;
I looked for islands, sought the river beds,
The child, the dove, and could not understand.

Rose Sonnets

Die schönen Wunder

Die schönen Wunder aus den sieben Reichen,
Die bald Zitronenfalter, groß an Stielen,
Bald Zwergflamingos, die in Büsche fielen,
Bald Muscheln sind aus zauberstillen Teichen,

O meine Rosen. Herzen. Mögt ihr bleichen,
Erschlafft, erschöpft von weißen Sonnenspielen,
Verzehrt vom Überschwang, dem Allzuvielen;
Tragt singend euch zu Grabe, süße Leichen!

Ich will euch doch vom lieben Zweig nicht trennen,
Euch nicht im engen, lauen Glase wissen,
Die kurze Spanne Blühn euch kunstreich dehnen.

O gut: an unermeßnem Glanz verbrennen,
Statt, von der heißen Erde fortgerissen,
Ein langes schales Leben hinzusehnen.

The Fairest Wonders

The fairest wonders from the seven zones,
That now are butterflies on stems that sway,
Now seashells out of magic silent bays,
Now dwarf-flamingoes set among the stones.

Oh you, my roses. Hearts. Though you be thrown
To earth by wilting, white-hot sunlight's rays,
Consumed with ecstasy in raging days,
Still hasten singing to the grave alone!

I will not cut you, will not make you tame,
Imprison you in narrow, tepid glass,
Nor will prolong the moment of your bloom.

Oh good: to burn in boundless, blinding flame,
And not be sundered from the earth and grass
To languish long within an empty room.

Mulattenrose

Mulattenrose. Mischling. Sinnt dein Blut
Bemalte Götzen noch, geschnitzte Waffen,
Das Rosabraun der starken Mantelaffen
In silbriggrau geschwellter Mähnenflut?

Du schattest nicht dein Antlitz vor der Glut
Mit grünen Händen. Weil dich Glut geschaffen.
Du hältst dich auf, den Sonnentrank zu raffen,
Die schöne Mulde, drin er schwebend ruht.

Dann steigt ein anders zarteres Erröten
Dir scheu, ganz leise unter wilde Braun.
Am Abendrain verflockt das Spiel der Lämmer,

Tönt letzter Amsel dunkelsamtnes Flöten.
Ein blonder Schopf durchschlüpft den Heckenzaun
Und ferne lischt sein Knabenschritt im Dämmer.

Mulatto Rose

Mulatto rose. A half-breed. In your veins
Your blood dreams painted idols, chiseled blades,
And strong baboons in dusky jungle glades,
With rose-brown flesh and silver flowing manes.

You bend aloft to drink the blazing rain.
Because it was from heat that you were made,
Your green hands do not hide your face in shade,
But hold a basin where the sun has lain.

Then, shyly, underneath your wild brown eyes,
Another redness rises in your cheeks.
On evening's edge the flocks break up their play.

The last bird utters somber velvet cries.
A blond-haired boy runs past along the creek,
And in the dark his footsteps die away.

Die Rose in der Nacht

Hadley

Sie glüht. Und ihre Haare kriechen groß
Auf blutrot dumpfen Sammet, schwarze Schlangen.
Sie neigt sich müd in duftendem Verlangen,
Die reife Frau. Und ist ein Herz doch bloß,

Ein heißes, sanftes Herz. Und birst, ein Schoß,
Der Liebe auf, den Himmel zu empfangen.
Und wird ein Antlitz mit gemalten Wangen.
Wenn Abend meerwärts fährt auf braunem Floß,

Ein Totenkauz im Düster greinend lacht,
Dann schlägt es tiefe Augen auf und wacht
Und fängt den Männertraum auf seinem Fluge.

Und sinkt schon morgen welk, am Strauch, im Kruge,
Und stand als eine Rose in der Nacht.
Die dunkelrote Rose in der Nacht.

Rose in the Night

Hadley

She glows. Her heavy strands of black hair slide
Like serpents over somber, blood-red plush.
She bends with passion scented sweet and lush,
A woman in full bloom, all sense and pride,

All burning, gentle heart. She opens wide
Her womb of love, wherein the heavens rush,
Becomes a face with painted cheeks that blush.
When twilight's raft drifts seaward with the tide,

The owl of death laughs in the fading light,
And opens deep, round eyes; then starts its flight
To hunt on midnight air the dreams of men.

And drops at morning wilted on the stem,
And stood there as a rose within the night.
The dark-red rose so deep within the night.

Orangengesicht

Angèle Pernet

Ein Süden. Schwere Seiden um die Lende
Wie Glanzgefieder wilder Papageien
Mit scharlachroten, safrangelben Schreien.
Weib. Braun und golden tasten ihre Brände.

Ihr Scheitel trägt das Kosen glühnder Hände
Wie Bürde durch der Palmen Fächelreihen
Zu Brunnen, die kristallnes Wasser speien,
In kleine Säle, deren kühle Wände

Doch still von großen Nächten überrinnen,
Da, Ströme, ihre schwarzen Haare blauen,
Der goldgebogne Ring in ihrem Ohre

An fremder Lippe klingt, aus ihren Sinnen
Sich lautlos heben die entzückten Klauen
Und trägen Schwingen riesiger Kondore.

Orange Face

Angèle Pernet

The South. And heavy silks surround her thighs
And gleam like plumes a wild parrot shows,
With scarlet screams where saffron yellow glows.
A girl: with brown and golden burning eyes.

Her hand bears warm caresses, tender sighs
Like burdens through the palm-trees' fanning rows
To fountains where the crystal water flows
To tiny halls where cool walls rise high,

But still with wondrous evenings overflow,
When streams wash blue her raven-colored hair,
And on her ears the golden-bending rings

Are brushed by strangers' lips, and when she knows
That silently enchanted talons tear
And giant condors spread their languid wings.

Chinesische Rose

Souvenir de Claudius Pernet

Im Gedenken an Siao Wan Ping

Ein Beet: ein Schatz von köstlichen Gewändern,
Da jedes leise seine Heimat rauscht,
Und dies, das Grün mit mattem Golde tauscht,
Ist deine Jacke aus den gelben Ländern

Mit weiten Ärmeln und bestickten Rändern:
Ein roter Zweig, ein Blumenantlitz lauscht,
Wenn großer Seidenrock sich knisternd bauscht
In Falten, die Jahrhunderte nicht ändern.

Und abends sang das Holz an deinen Lippen,
Die braune Flöte, dumpfen Marsch ins Fahle,
Und dies dein Liebeslied vom Weidenblatt

Glitt, wie verirrter Schwalbenflug um Klippen,
Um fremde Türme grauer Kathedrale
In fremder alter eingenickter Stadt.

Chinese Rose

Souvenir de Claudius Pernet
In memory of Siao Wan Ping

Like priceless garments: roses in the sand
That whisper of their homelands thousandfold.
This blossom, bending green with faded gold
Becomes your jacket from the yellow lands.

With open sleeves, edged with embroidered bands:
A ruby stem, a flower face beholds
When silken fabric billows and unfolds
With wrinkles that the centuries withstand.

The wood upon your lips sang in the night,
The bark-brown flute blew ballads dark as wine,
And like a willow leaf your lovesong's sound

Soared round the cliffs a wandering swallow's flight
Above exotic towers of graying shrines
Into a strange and ancient nodding town.

Rose Chiffon

Hugh Dickson

Ein junges Mädchen aus verklungner Zeit.
Mit Augen, die in Gärten immer schweifen
Wie zahme Rehe. Mit Karminsamtschleifen
An einem losen, sanften Schleierkleid

Von altem Rosa wie verschwommnes Leid.
Sie steigt zum Haus. Treppauf. Die Falbeln streifen
In mildem Gruß den Prankenhieb des Greifen,
Der steinern die Veranda überschreit.

Sie zieht ihr Ringlein ab mit roten Steinen,
Rückt silbern-grüner Damaststühle einen
Und setzt sich an das dämmernde Spinett,

Daß in den Park und Zwiegesang der Merlen
Durchs offne Fenster dünne Tropfen perlen
Aus einem kühlen, alten Menuett.

Chiffon Rose

Hugh Dickson

A lady from a time lost like a sound.
With eyes that wander tame as gentle does
Through garden groves. With crimson velvet bows
Upon a soft and flowing veiled gown,

Like vague remorse, of antique russet brown.
She climbs veranda steps, and as she goes
Her ruffles brush the griffon's taloned blow
That, poised in stone, protrudes above the ground.

She then removes her rings with scarlet jewels,
Adjusts a silver, damask-covered stool,
And sits before her spinet in the dark.

From windows icy pearls begin to sift,
An ancient minuet begins to drift,
And blends with blackbird voices in the park.

Milch

Frau Karl Druschki

Die großen Wolken fahren droben,
Ein Traumgebirg der Karawanken,
Mit wehend aufgerißnen Flanken,
Mit Gipfeln, wülstig und zerstoben.

Die großen Sphinxe lagern oben
Mit schlagend schwarzen Fluggedanken,
Die zottigen, bekrallten Pranken
Dem Abgrundsrande hingeschoben.

Und drunten weint in dumpfer Stunde
Das Kind, die Erde, zuckt und wittert
Nach ihrer Brüste dunklen Inseln.

Sie spalten auf; ein Tropfen splittert
Und knospt auf seinem durstgen Munde
Und blättert ab in weißem Rinnseln.

Milk

Frau Karl Druschki

The giant clouds are flying high
Imaginary Alpine chains
With tattered flanks and blowing manes
Where hilltops bulge and fragments fly.

The giant sphinxes rest on high;
Supreme in thoughts of flight they reign.
Their shaggy paws and talons strain
On precipices where they lie.

And down below, in dismal hours,
Toward a child, the earth, they bend
Their island-breasts that darkly gleam.

They open, and a drop descends.
Upon his mouth there blooms a flower
Whose petals fall in milky streams.

Liebe

Captain Harvey-Cant

Im Gedenken an K. J.

Ja, neige, neige dich, du Rosenrot,
Du kleine Ampel, Alabasterstern!
Dir will ich dienen, meinem Ruhm und Herrn,
Dir Opfer bieten, Wein und süßes Brot.

O nimm mich ein. Ich führe, sanftes Boot,
Mit deinem Wind in tiefen Abend gern;
Er wiegt dich sacht, und du bist doch schon fern
Und gleitest scheinend nieder in den Tod.

So ohne Flackern schwindest du, o Licht,
So sinkst du, Nachen, ohne Hilfeschrei.
Ich hör dein Schweigen: hör den Jammer nicht,

Ich seh dich an: die Erde rollt vorbei.
Du bist gestorben, Sommertagsgesicht;
Ich lebe, daß ich trauern mag: verzeih.

Love

Captain Harvey-Cant
In memory of K. J.

Bend down to me, bend down oh deep rose red,
You tiny lamp, you alabaster star,
I want to serve you, oh my lord, my czar,
And bring you offerings of wine and bread.

Receive me now. Your gentle boat I've led
Before the wind, across the evening's bar;
It sways you softly, yet you move afar,
And fade away, perhaps already dead.

A steady flame, oh light, you disappear;
Thus, little boat, you sink without a cry.
I hear your silence; grief I cannot hear.

I look at you and watch the earth roll by.
Now that you've gone, my summer day, my dear,
I live that I may mourn to see you die.

Prussian Coats of Arms

Wappen von Allenburg

Ein rotes Elchhaupt auf Silbergrund, aus grünem Röhricht steigend

Ich geh durch Erde, die schon nicht mehr ist;
Denn meine Erde ist nur Teil von mir,
Wie ich mit Schaufel, Haupt und Widerrist
Ein blödes, grauses, ungeschlachtes Tier.

Sie klatscht um meine Kniee als ein Sumpf,
Hängt von der trägen Lippe als ein Schlamm,
Hockt, Nebelschlange, feucht am roten Rumpf,
Schiebt unters Maul den flechtenblassen Stamm.

Ich bin, die war, die ferngestorbne Zeit,
Die wüst im großen Wäldermoor gehaust,
In tiefe Flocken Wölfe hingeschneit,
Mit dunklem Sturm den Uhu hergebraust.

Ich bin das Wilde, Dumpfe, das man schlug,
Das man erschlagen, weil es fremd und stumm;
Was schlau und müde Karren schleppt und Pflug,
Dem legt der Mörder bunten Halsschmuck um.

Mir ward, die ihre Öde klagt und schnarrt,
Die Nacht des Raben freundlich zugesellt,
Die im Geröhre ächzt, in Birken knarrt
Und vor dem Licht der warmen Dörfer hält.

Mir ward ein Regenhimmel, graulich schwer,
Der zäh und stickig niederplumpt ins Luch,

Allenburg

On a silver ground, a red elk's
head emerges from green reeds.

I tread forgotten earth now long deceased;
For this lost land is but a part of me,
A shy and clumsy, terrifying beast,
With haunches, head, and shovel-antlered tree.

It laps about my knees, a murky swamp,
Hangs from my sluggish lips like dripping phlegm,
Wraps 'round red flanks a snake of fog and damp,
And feeds my mouth the lichen-crusted stem.

I am what was, the far departed age
That, wild, in giant wooded moors once housed,
That blew the wolves along when blizzards raged,
And, dark with storms, the sleeping owls once roused.

I am the dumb, the wild, the things now dead
That men have killed for being mute and strange,
That dragged the heavy plough and spurred the sled,
Adorned by murderers with charming chains.

And when the barren darkness wailed and moaned,
I was the friend of ravens in the night,
Who rasped in reeds and in the birches groaned,
And halted at the villages' warm light.

For me the rainy sky, whose heavy gray
Fell thick and stifling down upon the fen,

Das Fell am Leib, an meinem Hirn die Wehr,
Nicht Hand noch Peitsche, Stall und Trog und Tuch.

Das tierisch Mächtige hat sie entsetzt,
Das arglos Fromme meuchelt ihre List:
Daß es verende, wund und tot gehetzt,
Die Erdenkindheit. Die doch nicht mehr ist.

Became my fur, my antlers' stiff array—
Not hand, not whip, nor stall, nor trough, nor pen.

The mighty beasts struck terror into man.
With cunning tricks he hunted innocence,
And wounded it, and slew it as it ran:
In earthly childhood. That has passed long since.

Wappen von Bocholt

Auf grünem Grund eine silberne Buche

Einmal bin ich in die Welt gegangen:
Blumen lachten, wie die Quellen sangen,
Vor der Scheune tanzten Spatzenschwärme,
Brot und Sonne schien voll goldner Wärme.

Doch dann fiel ich von der Menschen Wegen,
Unter Tieren hab ich lang gelegen;
Kam der Engerling, mich anzustaunen,
Fand der Maulwurf her, mir zuzuraunen.

Als die Augenäpfel mir verdarben,
Schwanden zart getuschte Wangenfarben,
Beinern blieb vom Bilde nur der Rahmen.
Aber nieder sanken Kern und Samen.

Bin in jene Frucht ich eingekrochen?
Hab ich jene Schale dann zerbrochen?
Sprang ich fort von meiner eignen Hüfte,
Da ich silbern aufwuchs in die Lüfte?

Als der Tag die Sonne mitgenommen,
Ist ein armer schwacher Hund gekommen.
Jeder hetzt ihn, keiner will ihn haben;
Der ihn liebte, wurde längst begraben.

Zitternd leckt er seiner Wunde Rinnseln
Und beklagt sich scheu mit leisem Winseln,
Bis mein Arm ihn wärmt in grünem Tuche
Und mein Antlitz aus der Silberbuche.

Bocholt

On a green ground a silver beech tree

Once I went into the world:
Flowers laughed and fountains swirled;
By the barn danced sparrow-swarms;
Bread and sun were golden warm.

Then I fell from human ways;
Long with animals I lay.
Came the grub to watch and hear,
Moles to whisper in my ear.

When at last my eyes decayed,
Soft-hued flesh began to fade,
My picture left a frame of bone.
But far above the seeds were sown.

Did I creep into the fruit?
Break the rind, invade the root?
Did I spring forth from my thigh
And rise silvery to the sky?

Once when sun had gone with day
There came a poor, weak dog my way,
Chased, unwanted, never fed;
The one who loved him long was dead.

Trembling, shy, he licks his wounds,
Whimpers sadly. But is soon
Warmed beneath green robes I reach
Round him from the silver beech.

Wappen von Elmshorn

In Rot auf Wellen ein altertümliches silbernes Segelschiff

Unsre Mutter schreitet durch die Flut,
Fleht mit Masten Stern und Wind vom Blau,
Günstge Sterne, Winde kindergut,
Mit den Heiligenarmen einer Frau.

Ihre Tage fahren über Meer,
Pflügen ewig grauen Ozean,
Ihre Nächte, leuchtturmkarg und hehr,
Sind Planetensprüchen untertan.

Schwarzer Schattenstreif umkrampft den Bug,
Wirft sie hin auf dampfend nasses Bett;
Schwer in Schäumen keucht ihr Atemzug;
Roter Fruchtschatz schwillt ihr unterm Brett.

Wenn ihr dann der bunten Muschel lauscht,
Ihrem algengrünen Haar enttropft,
Wißt ihr, daß ein Wiegenlied sie rauscht,
Und den Herzschlag, der durch Planken klopft.

Elmshorn

On red, over waves, an old-fashioned
silver sailing ship.

Our mother forges through the seas,
And prays with masts to ward off harm,
For lucky stars, a gentle breeze,
With saintly, outstretched, woman's arms.

Her days traverse the sea and sky
And plough eternal waves of gray;
Her lighthouse-barren nights rise high,
Enthralled by words the planets say.

A shadow wave enfolds her brow
And plunges her in beds of cold;
In foam she heaves her gasping bow,
And red fruit treasures swell her hold.

And from the seashell at your ear,
Lost by her hair so green and dank,
Her whispered lullaby you hear,
And beating heart beneath the planks.

Wappen von Frauenburg

In Rot eine silberne Burg mit verschlossenem Tor; auf dem mittelsten der drei Zinnentürme steht ein Weib mit gefalteten Händen

Ich halte die Hände rund gewölbt zu einer Schale,
Daß in sie niederfalle ein Tropfen vom himmlischen Mahle.

Ich habe so lange schon müde und hoffend gewartet,
Wolkenfetzen im Haar, vom Blitz die Wange zerschartet.

Unter mir kreiselt Fahrzeug, Filmvolk und hohe Ziffer,
Über mir steigt und surrt und stürzt der eilende Schiffer.

Menschen schreiben viel Bücher, üben viel Morde;
Springer und Ringer und Redner: die Welt schmaust
Rekorde.

Nur das Brot haben goldene Messer sehr ungleich
geschnitten;
Ich seh es vom weißen Turme: ich steh ja inmitten.

Aber die unten finden mich nicht im Schaffen und Machen,
Und die oben erspähen mich klein, so bittend, und lachen.

Und doch weiß ich: Wenn Jeder den Andern ins Grab
zertreten,
Werden über den Gräbern meine Hände stehen und beten.

Frauenburg

On red a silver castle with a closed
gate; upon the central of three towers
stands a woman with folded hands.

I cup my hands together like a bowl
To catch ambrosial drops to feed my soul.

I've hoped and waited long, am tired and weak,
With cloud-wisped hair and lightning-furrowed cheek.

Below rush cars and film-stars, high statistics.
Above me sailors soar on grand ballistics.

And many publish books, and many die.
A feast of records towers to the sky.

And golden bread-knives cut unequal shares.
I stand between and judge it is unfair.

Below they see me not, but work and fight.
To those above I'm laughable and slight.

And yet I know, when none are left to slay,
Above the graves my hands will stand and pray.

Wappen von Lassan

Auf blauem, sternübersätem Grunde
ein steigender silberner Fisch

Über die Teiche schreiten unbeschuhte Frauen.
Wie mögen Menschenfrauen über die Wasser gehn?
Sie tragen lichtgeflochtenes Netzwerk in Händen
Und ragen mächtiger, wenn sie, es aufwärtszusenden,
Geschwungenen Arms auf rinnendem Spiegel stehn.

Denn Fische schweben durch die blauen Gebreite.
Wo flattern Fische auf mit Nachtkauz und Triel?
Ihre Flossen klingen silbern an, da sie steigen.
Manchmal rasten sie droben auf Ahornzweigen;
Sie jagten den flirrenden Stern im Zenit, bis er niederfiel.

Die silbernen Fische singen über Ländern und Meeren.
Wann finget ihr Fische je, und sie waren nicht stumm?
Orf und Schmerle schweigen. Sie aber, ohne Namen,
Streuen überallhin ihrer Töne Rieselsamen,
Der die Weltkugel füllt wie blitzendes Bienengesumm.

Eine Stunde sitzt abends bei euch am Fenster.
Wer hat nicht umsonst schon die bleibende Stunde erhofft?
Und nun kommt sie und teilt die schlichte Kost eurer
    Tische,
Und sie lehrt euch vielleicht das Lied der singenden Fische.
Ja, sie kommt: einmal. Nicht oft.

Lassan

On a blue ground strewn with
stars a climbing silver fish.

Over the ponds stride barefoot women.
Are they mortal, is it water over which they pass?
In their hands they carry nets of woven light,
And, towering, fling them aloft with all their might,
Then stand with outstretched arms on the rippling glass.

For the fish are soaring through the bluish breadths.
Do fish flap skyward with owls and loons?
As they climb their fins make silvery ringing sounds.
Sometimes they rest in maple boughs high off the ground;
They chased the flickering star from zenith down behind
the moon.

The silver fishes sing across land and sea.
Have you ever caught a fish that was not dumb?
Perch and pike keep silent. But they, the nameless breed
Are spreading everywhere their voices' sifting seed
That fills the earth-sphere with a blinking beehive hum.

An hour sits with you one evening by the window.
Who has not hoped for an hour to last forever?
But now it comes and shares your simple meal and simple
wishes,
And teaches you, perhaps, the song of the singing fishes.
Yes, it comes: sometimes. But hardly ever.

Wappen von Neidenburg

Silber; ein wilder Mann mit Laubschurz und Blätterkrone, der zwischen zwei grünen Stauden auf Rasengrund tritt, ein geschwungenes Schwert in der rechten Hand, eine Goldlilie in der linken

Drüben roden sie die Wälder;
Mit den Rodern will ich fechten,
Diesen Gott in meiner Linken,
Dieses Erz in meiner Rechten.

Segen träuft die goldne Blume,
Und sie heiligt meine Waffen;
Denn Gebete bring ich allem,
Was ich selber nicht erschaffen.

Sieh der Mücke kleines Leben,
Und wie ist es leicht zu töten;
Kannst sie doch aus Lehm nicht kneten,
Kannst sie nicht aus Weide flöten.

Nur zuweilen rüttelt Hunger:
Mürbes Fleisch ist gut zu essen,
Und wie ich den Eber morde,
Werden mich die Wölfe fressen.

Dennoch bleibt mir freund und willig,
Was sich duckt in Busch und Quadern;
Weise Schlange nennt mir Kräuter,
Kröte die metallnen Adern.

Neidenburg

Silver; a wild-man with leafy crown
and apron stands on grassy ground
between two bushes, a sword in his
right hand, a golden lily in his left.

Over there they clear the forest;
With the woodmen I will fight,
With this god held in my left hand,
With this metal in my right.

Blessing brings my golden flower,
And it sanctifies my blade;
Prayers I give to all creation:
Everything I have not made.

See the tiny cricket's life.
See how easily you take it.
But its form you cannot carve,
And from clay you cannot make it.

Sometimes I am moved by hunger:
Tender flesh is good to eat.
As the boar becomes my victim,
I become the wolf-pack's meat.

Yet they still remain my brothers:
All the things that creep and soar.
Serpents show me herbs and potions,
Toads uncover veins of ore.

Brüder hausen fern in Städten,
Wo sie schlachten, spielen, rauchen.
Da ist vieles, was sie haben,
Und ist wenig, was sie brauchen.

Denn schon mir ward Überreiches:
Spieß und Pfeile, wenn ich jage,
Und ein Weib für meine Nächte
Und ein Kind für meine Tage.

Zu den Wurzeln mag ich fallen
Aus dem Kampfe mit den Rodern:
In der gleichen Erde werden
Einstmals ihre Knochen modern.

Kinsmen live in distant cities
Where they play and kill and feed.
They have many fine possessions,
But so little that they need.

But I now have more than riches:
Spears and arrows when I slay,
And a woman for my nighttime,
And a child to fill my day.

Soon I may fall to the tree-roots,
Murdered by the woodmen's shot.
But beneath the same dark soil
Someday soon their bones will rot.

Wappen von Schloppe

Auf schwarzem Grund eine goldene Krone, unter der Krone drei silberne Sterne und unter den Sternen ein silberner Sichelmond

In schwarzem Laube schwellen die Gestirne.
Erst wenn sie faulen, stürzt der Himmel ein.
Dann schmilzt der Mond vor Quittenfrucht und Birne
Und mischt dem Frühtau seinen blassen Wein.

Auf öden Feldern wachsen noch Dämonen.
Die Tote jagen, reiten nachts den Wind,
Und andre ziehn aus Sümpfen ihre Kronen,
Die triefend schwer von Schleim und Schnecken sind.

Die Echse weint. Aus ihren Kinderblicken
Tropft goldengrün ein glänzender Smaragd,
Zersprüht im Moos mit zaghaft feinem Ticken
Am roten Hexenhaar der jungen Magd:

Sie liegt bei Tieren. Läßt die schmalen Hände
Dem blauen Werwolf, der sie hündisch leckt,
Und lächelt sanft, wenn ihre bleiche Lende
Der Geiermönch mit dunkler Kutte deckt.

Schloppe

On a black ground a golden crown, under
the crown three silver stars and under
the stars a silver crescent moon.

From leafy blackness clustered star-fruits stare,
And when they rot the sky will crumble through.
The moon will melt along with quince and pear,
And mix its pale wine with the morning dew.

The demons breed and grow on barren ground.
Those who pursue the dead ride midnight gales,
And others pull from swamps their golden crowns
That drip with heavy mire and slimy snails.

The lizard weeps. And from her childlike eye
A gleaming emerald drips down golden green
Into the moss, and splatters, crackling dry,
The red hair of the witches' maiden queen:

She lies with animals, and gently sighs
When werewolves, doglike, lick her hands and howl,
And smiles as, rising dark above her thighs,
The monkish vulture spreads his somber cowl.

Wappen von Usedom

Auf rotem Grunde ein silberner Fischgreif
(Greif, dessen Leib in einem Fischschwanze endigt)

Alle Bäume haben ästige Kronen,
Alle Brunnen haben tiefen Schacht;
Kann ich nicht in den allertiefsten mehr wohnen,
Flügle ich phosphorleuchtend auf in Nacht,
Wenn die Tode weiß
Und kristallenes Eis
Zuckerig hart in ihren Kiefern kracht.

Dunstig trägt mein Atem, eine Säule,
Plumpen Mond, der nur eine Scheibe Ton,
Furchtsam dienert in meinen Schatten die Eule,
Türme peitscht meines Flossenschweifs blitzender Hohn.
Unter schwebenden Schnee,
Über taumelnde See
Heben versteinerte Wogenkämme den Thron.

Selber bin ich das kalte silberne Feuer;
Drei Elemente öffnen mir den Palast:
Erde! Ich bin ein Katzenspuk im Gemäuer.
Wasser! Ich bin ein Fisch im gläsernen Glast.
Himmel, in deinem Hirn
Bin ich Gewölk und Gestirn,
Das deine Lüfte in schleifenden Nebeln verpraßt.

Opfre ich mich auf schäumenden Altars Stufe,
Weil Tiere schwach und Menschen zu kümmerlich,
Schleudre ich in Ewigkeiten schweigende Rufe,

Usedom

On a red ground a silver fish-griffon
(griffon whose body ends in a fishtail)

All the trees have branching crowns;
All the wells are deep and black;
If I cannot live underground
I trail aloft a phosphorescent track,
When death is white
In crystal night
And, sugared hard with ice, the pinetrees crack.

Upon my breath, a foggy tower,
I bear the bulky moon, a disc of clay;
Within my shadow frightened owls cower;
Beneath my lashing tail the turrets sway.
In blowing snow
The surging sea below
Uplifts my throne on frozen waves and spray.

I am the fire, a cold and silvery light.
Three elements ignite beneath my rays:
Earth! I am the cat who haunts the night.
Water! I'm the fish in glistening glaze.
Sky! Within your brain
I am the clouds and rain
That hide your winds in fog and smothering haze.

And when, upon the altar, I must die,
Because the beast is weak and man too small,
And send the universe a silent cry,

Singen aus Ewigkeiten Welten für mich.
Als ich den Nacken bog,
Bebte Festland und sog
Seine Städte: Nichts ist größer denn ich.

Eternal worlds will echo back my call.
And when I bend my neck
The shaking earth will wreck
Its cities: I am greatest. I am all.

Worlds

Zueignung

Sie nahm den Silberstift
Und hieß ihn hingehn über die weiße matt glänzende Fläche:
Ihr Land. Er zog
Und schuf Berge.
Kahle Berge, nackte kantig steinerne Gipfelstirnen, über
Öde sinnend;
Ihre Leiber
Schwanden umhüllt, vergingen hinter dem bleichen Gespinst
Einer Wolke.
So hing das Bild vor dem schwarzen Grunde, und Menschen
sahen es an.
Und Menschen sprachen:
»Wo ist Duft? Wo ist Saft, gesättigter Schimmer?
Wo das strotzende, kraftvoll springende Grün der Ebenen
Und der Klippe bräunlich verbranntes Rot oder ihr taubes
graues Düster?
Kein spähender Falke rüttelt, hier flötet kein Hirt.
Nie tönen groß in milderes Abendblau die schön
geschwungenen Hörner wilder Ziegen.
Farbenlos, wesenlos ist dies, ohne Stimme; es redet zu uns
nicht.
Kommt weiter.«

Sie aber stand und schwieg.
Klein, unbeachtet stand sie im Haufen, hörte und schwieg.
Nur ihre Schulter zuckte, ihr Blick losch in Tränen.
Und die Wolke, die ihre zeichnende Hand geweht,

Dedication

She took the silver shaft
And bade it travel out across the white, dull-shining plain:
Her land. It roamed
And wrought mountains.
Barren mountains, naked, jagged summit-brows of stone that brooded over deserts;
Their bodies
Disappeared enshrouded, lost behind the faded cobwebs
Of a cloud.
And so the image stood before a darkened background, and was seen by men.
And men began to speak:
"Where is fragrance? Flesh and blood? Or glowing richness?
Where is the strong, springing green of luxuriant plains
And the scorched russet brown of the cliffs, or their shadowy gray?
No spying falcon hovers, no shepherd blows his flute.
The finely curved horns of wild goats never sound their note abroad on mild blue evenings.
This has no color, no substance, no voice; this does not speak to us
Let us move on."

She, however, stood and said nothing.
Small, unnoticed, she stood in the crowd, listened, and said nothing.
Only her shoulder twitched; tears drowned her sight.
And the cloud that sailed from her inscribing hand

Senkte sich und umwallte, hob und trug sie empor
Zum Schrund ihrer kahlen Berge.
Ein Wartender,
Dem zwei grüngoldene Basilisken den Kronreif schlangen,
Stand im Dämmer auf, glomm und neigte sich, sie zu grüßen.

Sank down and swirled around her, lifted her, and carried
her aloft
To the clefts of her barren mountains.
A male figure, waiting,
Two green-golden basilisks wrung round his crown,
Arose in the gloom, glowed dim, and bowed to greet her.

Die Stadt

Sie gingen
Durch den nebelleicht kühlen Wintermorgen, Liebende,
Hand in Hand.
Erde bröckelte hart, gefrorene Pfütze sprang gläsern unter
den Sohlen.
Drunten am Uferwege
Saß einer in brauner Sammetjoppe vor seiner Staffelei
Und malte die blattlos hängende Weide.
Kinder pirschten neugierig näher,
Und die Großen hielten für Augenblicke mit ihrem Gange
ein, tadelten, lobten.
An dem algengrünen, glitschigen Stege
Schwamm ein lecker, verrotteter Kahn.
Drei Schwäne über den Wellen
Bogen die stengelschlanken Hälse, schweigend, entfalteten
sich, blühten.
Die Frau brach Brot und warf es weit in die Flut.

Unter starrenden Eichen,
Die Äste, schwarz, verrenkt, wie gemarterte Glieder
streckten,
Schritten sie an den fröstelnden Rasen, efeuumwucherten
Pfeilern verschlossener Gärten dahin.
Als sie die lange steinerne Brücke betraten,
Riß Sonne den Nebel von sich wie ein Gewand,
Und die Stadt stieg auf, schräg hinter dem breiten Becken
des Flusses.
Ineinander, übereinander schoben sich Dächer, schwarzgrau
glänzend wie Dohlengefieder, einzelne, höhere
patinagrün; goldene Turmhauben blitzten.

The City

They walked
Into the cool, foggy winter morning—lovers, hand in hand.
Hard earth crumbled, frozen puddles shattered glassy underfoot.
Down at the water's edge
A man in a brown velvet jacket sat before his easel
And painted the leafless, hanging willow tree.
Curious children crept closer,
And the lovers paused a moment in their walk to blame and praise.
Beside the moss-green, slippery bridge
A leaky, rotting rowboat lay.
Three swans above the waves
Bent stemlike necks and silently unfolded wings and bloomed.
The woman broke some bread and threw it far from shore.

Beneath towering oaks
That stretched their branches, black and out of joint like martyred arms,
They strode past frosty lawns and the ivy-covered columns of closed gardens.
When they reached the long stone bridge
The sun threw off its robe of fog
And the city rose up steep behind the widespread basin of the river.
Roofs stood shuffled, stacked upon each other, shining blackish gray like jackdaws' feathers, some with green patina rising higher; golden hoods of towers gleamed.

Möwen umkreischten, hungrig flatternde Bettler, das
Brückengeländer.
Sie waren hinüber
Und schauten vor mürrisch alltäglichem Hause den Knaben
zu, die ihrem gelben Hund die wunde, blutende Pfote
verbanden.
Frauen mit Marktnetzen, Henkelkörben blickten vorüber-
eilend die müßigen Fremden knapp und mißtrauisch an,
Verschwanden hinter den Türen düsterer kleiner murkliger
Läden.

Lauter und stärker, wohlhäbiger, fülliger wurden die
Straßen.
Stattliche Gasthöfe luden mit kräftigen Lettern ein;
Rötliche Backsteinmauern standen machtvoll-gewichtig da
gleich Ratsherren alter Zeit mit Puffenwams und
Barett und prunkender Schaube.
Bahnen lärmten fröhlich, bimmelten flink, wie ein Gassen-
junge am Parktor, entwischten.
Männer in dicken, warmen Mänteln beredeten rauchend
und lebhaft schreitend Handel und Wandel,
Und bald fing die Garküche an, ihren Stand mit nahrhaften
Bratgerüchen zu rühmen.
Laden reihte an Laden sich,
Bot zartes, saftiges Fleisch und Wildbret, Fische, geräucher-
ten Aal und Sprotten,
Bot knusprig braunes längliches Brot, süß, mit Korinthen
gefüllt, und herbes, das mehlüberstäubt oder mit Salz
und Kümmel bestreut war.
Zwischen zwei Kupferbechern duckte ein winziges chine-
sisches Teehaus von kirschrot gelacktem Holze sein
geschweiftes vergoldetes Dach.

Circling seagulls screamed, hungry flapping beggars, round the bridge's railing.
Then they were across,
And watched before a sullen, ordinary house as boys bound up the wounded paw of a yellow dog.
Women rushing by with shopping nets and baskets gave the strangers brief, suspicious glances,
And then disappeared behind the doors of dingy little shops.

The street grew louder, full of crowds, and prosperous.
Stately restaurants lured them in with dark, bold lettering;
And red brick walls stood ponderous and strong, like senators of olden times with pleated doublets, caps, and splendid ruffs.
The streetcars rattled cheerfully, and clanging, quick, went scurrying like urchins at the entrance to the park.
Men in thick, warm overcoats walked smoking, talking eagerly of times and trade,
A sausage wagon advertised its wares with steaming roasted smells.
Row upon row of stores
That offered tender, juicy meat, and game, and fish, and herring, and smoked eel,
And long, brown, crunchy bread—some sweet and filled with currants, some tart and strewn with flour, salt, or caraway.
Between two copper urns a tiny Chinese teahouse of lacquered, cherry-crimson wood, was ducked beneath a curving, golden roof.

Doch das Gewölb, da um teures Geld Tränke und Salben
und Pulver gemengt und verabreicht werden,
Wies durchs Fenster den Greis, wie lebend, gebückt im
Sessel,
In wollener Kutte, mit schlohweiß wallendem Bart;
Er schloß die Lider.
Hinter ihm grinste ein langes scheußliches Beingeripp mit
Totenschädels höhnischen Augenhöhlen und Zähnen,
Die glitzernde Sense in einer Hand und mit der andern des
Sinkenden Schulter krallend.
Eine Uhr zeigte Mitternacht.
Da erschrak die Frau und griff nach dem Manne —

Er nickte und lächelte aber;
Denn er sah nichts als ihr finsteres Haar und ihr blasses
dunkeläugiges Antlitz.

But toward the chamber where expensive potions, powders, salves were mixed and sold
There pointed through the glass an aged man, as if alive, bent over in his chair,
And wore a woolen cowl and had a flowing, snow-white beard;
His eyes were closed.
Behind him stood a tall, appalling skeleton with mocking, skull-deep eyes and grinning teeth,
The gleaming sickle in one hand, the other clawed around the old man's sinking shoulder.
A clock showed midnight.
The woman shivered, reaching out to touch the man—

He merely nodded, smiled.
For he saw nothing but the blackness of her hair and the pallor of her dark-eyed face.

Der Engel im Walde

Gib mir deine Hand, die liebe Hand, und komm mit mir;
Denn wir wollen hinweggehen von den Menschen.
Sie sind klein und böse, und ihre kleine Bosheit haßt und peinigt uns.
Ihre hämischen Augen schleichen um unser Gesicht, und ihr gieriges Ohr betastet das Wort unseres Mundes.
Sie sammeln Bilsenkraut . . .
So laß uns fliehn
Zu den sinnenden Feldern, die freundlich mit Blumen und Gras unsere wandernden Füße trösten,
An den Strom, der auf seinem Rücken geduldig wuchtende Bürden, schwere, güterstrotzende Schiffe trägt,
Zu den Tieren des Waldes, die nicht übelreden.

Komm.
Herbstnebel schleiert und feuchtet das Moos mit dumpf smaragdenem Leuchten.
Buchenlaub rollt, Reichtum goldbronzener Münzen.
Vor unseren Schritten springt, rote zitternde Flamme, das Eichhorn auf.
Schwarze gewundene Erlen züngeln am Pfuhl empor in kupfriges Abendglasten.

Komm.
Denn die Sonne ist nieder in ihre Höhle gekrochen, und ihr warmer rötlicher Atem verschwebt.
Nun tut ein Gewölb sich auf.
Unter seinem graublauen Bogen zwischen bekrönten Säulen der Bäume wird der Engel stehn,
Hoch und schmal, ohne Schwingungen.

The Angel in the Forest

Give me your hand, beloved, and follow me,
And we will go away from men.
For they are petty, they are wicked, and their petty wickedness detests and torments us.
Their spiteful eyes prowl round our faces and their greedy ears defile the words that pass our lips.
They harvest deadly nightshade . . .
So let us flee
Unto the musing fields that will console our wandering feet with friendly flowers and grass,
Unto the river, bearing patiently upon its back the weighty burden of the full, freight-laden ships,
Unto the forest animals that speak no ill.

Come.
The autumn fog enshrouds and saturates the moss with gloomy emerald glow.
Beech leaves drift, a treasure of gold-bronze coins.
Before our feet a red squirrel leaps and flickers like a flame.
Black, twisted alder trees shoot up beside a pond into the coppery sheen of evening.

Come.
For the sun has crept down in its cave; its warm red breath has blown away.
And now a vaulted chamber opens wide.
Beneath its gray-blue arches, by the broad-crowned columns of the trees, will stand the angel.
Tall and thin, devoid of wings.

Sein Antlitz ist Leid.
Und sein Gewand hat die Bleiche eisig blinkender Sterne
in Winternächten.
Der Seiende,
Der nicht sagt, nicht soll, der nur ist,
Der keinen Fluch weiß noch Segen bringt und nicht in
Städte hinwallt zu dem, was stirbt:
Er schaut uns nicht
In seinem silbernen Schweigen.
Wir aber schauen ihn,
Weil wir zu zweit und verlassen sind.

Vielleicht
Weht ein braunes, verwelktes Blatt an seine Schulter,
entgleitet;
Das wollen wir aufheben und verwahren, ehe wir
weiterziehn.

Komm, mein Freund, mit mir, komm.
Die Treppe in meines Vaters Haus ist dunkel und krumm
und eng, und die Stufen sind abgetreten;
Aber jetzt ist es das Haus der Waise, und fremde Leute
wohnen darin.
Nimm mich fort.
Schwer fügt der alte rostige Schlüssel im Tor sich meinen
schwachen Händen.
Nun knarrt es zu.
Nun sieh mich an in der Finsternis, du, von heut meine
Heimat.
Denn deine Arme sollen mir bergende Mauern baun,
Und dein Herz wird mir Kammer sein und dein Auge mein
Fenster, durch das der Morgen scheint.

His countenance is grief.
And his garment has the radiance of icy blinking stars on winter nights.
The One Who Is,
Who nothing says, nor blessing brings, nor visits those who die in towns:
He sees us not
Out of his silver stillness.
But we may look at him,
For we are two, and are alone.

Perhaps
A wilted russet leaf will fall from his shoulder;
This we must take and keep before we journey on.

Oh come, my friend, come with me.
The stairway in my father's house is dark and close and crooked, and its steps are worn;
But now it is an orphan's house where strangers live.
Take me away.
The ancient rusted key that locks the gate resists my feeble hands.
But now the hinges finally creak shut.
Now look at me in darkness—you, from this day on my home.
For your arms will build a sheltering wall about me,
And your heart will be my room, your eye my window where the morning shines.

Und es türmt sich die Stirn, da du schreitest.
Du bist mein Haus an allen Straßen der Welt, in jeder
Senke, auf jedem Hügel.
Du Dach, du wirst ermattet mit mir unter glühendem
Mittag lechzen, mit mir erschauern, wenn Schneesturm
peitscht.
Wir werden dürsten und hungern, zusammen erdulden,
Zusammen einst an staubigem Wegesrande sinken und
weinen . . .

Your forehead towers higher as you go.
You are my house in all the world's streets, in every valley and on every hill.
Oh you, my roof, will languish with me under burning noons and shudder in the snow.
And we will thirst and hunger and endure together,
And together someday on a dusty roadside we will fall and weep . . .

Aus dem Dunkel

Aus dem Dunkel komme ich, eine Frau.
Ich trage ein Kind und weiß nicht mehr, wessen;
Einmal hab ichs gewußt.
Aber nun ist kein Mann mehr für mich . . .
Alle sind hinter mir eingesunken wie Rinnsaal,
Das die Erde trank.
Ich gehe weiter und weiter.
Denn ich will vor Tag ins Gebirge, und die Gestirne
schwinden schon.

Aus dem Dunkel komme ich.
Durch finstere Gassen schritt ich einsam,
Da jäh vorstürzendes Licht mit Krallen die sanfte Schwärze
zerriß,
Der Pardel die Hirschkuh,
Und weit aufgestoßene Tür häßliches Kreischen, wüstes
Gejohle, tierisches Brüllen spie.
Trunkene wälzten sich . . .
Ich schüttelte das am Wege vom Saum meines Kleides.

Und ich wanderte über den verödeten Markt.
Blätter schwammen in Lachen, die den Mond spiegelten.
Magere, gierige Hunde berochen Abfälle auf den Steinen.
Früchte faulten zertreten,
Und ein Greis in Lumpen quälte noch immer sein armes
Saitenspiel
Und sang mit dünner, mißtönig klagender Stimme
Ungehört.
Und diese Früchte waren einst in Sonne und Tau gereift,
Träumend noch vom Duft und Glück der liebenden Blüte,

Out of Darkness

Out of darkness I come, a woman.
I carry a child, and have forgotten whose it is;
Once I knew.
But now there is no longer any man for me . . .
Behind me all of them have disappeared like rivulets
The earth drank dry.
And on I go and on.
Before the day I must be in the mountains, and already constellations fade.

Out of darkness I come.
Through shadowed streets I walked alone,
Then sudden, lunging light with talons ripped soft blackness,
As a panther fells a doe,
And a door flung wide spat ugly screams, demented howling, beastly cries.
And men rolled drunken in the street.
I shook them from my skirt as I walked past.

And then I crossed the empty marketplace.
Leaves swam in puddles where the moon was shining.
Emaciated, greedy dogs sniffed garbage on the stones.
Fruits rotted squashed;
An old man dressed in rags still bowed his poor, tormented strings
And raised his thin, discordant, mournful voice
Unheard.
Those fruits had once grown ripe in sun and dew,
In happy fragrant dreams of loving blooms,

Doch der wimmernde Bettler
Vergaß das längst und kannte nichts anderes mehr als
Hunger und Durst.

Vor dem Schlosse des Mächtigen stand ich still,
Und da ich die unterste Stufe trat,
Zerbarst der fleischrote Porphyr knackend an meiner
Sohle. –
Ich wendete mich
Und schaute empor zu dem kahlen Fenster, der späten
Kerze des Denkenden,
Der sann und sann und nie seiner Frage Erlösung fand,
Und zu dem verhüllten Lämpchen des Kranken, der doch
nicht lernte,
Wie er sterben sollte.
Unter dem Brückenbogen
Zankten zwei scheußliche Gerippe sich um Gold.
Ich hob meine Armut als grauen Schild vor mein Antlitz
Und zog ungefährdet vorbei.

Im Fernen redet der Fluß mit seinen Ufern.

Nun strauchle ich den steinigen, widerstrebenden Pfad
hinan.
Felsgeröll, Stachelsträucher verwunden die blinden,
tastenden Hände:
Eine Höhle wartet,
Die im tiefsten Geklüft den erzgrünen Raben herbergt,
der keinen Namen hat.
Da werde ich eingehn,
Unter dem Schutz der großen schattenden Schwinge mich
niederkauern und ruhn.

But the whimpering beggar
Had long ago forgotten this, and thought of nothing but his
hunger and his thirst.

Before the palace of the mighty I stood still,
And when I trod upon the lowest step
The flesh-red porphyry burst cracking underneath my
sole.—
I turned
And gazed aloft to barren windows, to the midnight candle
of the thinker,
Who pondered, pondered, but could not invent redemption
from his doubt,
And to the muffled lamp within the sickroom, where the
patient would not learn
How he should die.
Beneath the bridge
Two horrid skeletons disputed gold.
I raised the gray shield of my poverty before my face
And passed them by unharmed.

Now, far away, the river whispers to its banks.

And now I stumble forward on the stony, stubborn path.
Jumbled rocks and thistles wound my groping hands:
A cave awaits me
That conceals inside its deepest crack the bronze-green,
nameless raven.
I will enter
And crouch down to rest beneath the sheltering shadows of
his giant wings,

Verdämmernd dem stummen wachsenden Wort meines
Kindes lauschen
Und schlafen, die Stirn gen Osten geneigt,
Bis Sonnenaufgang.

And listen, drowsing, to the silent, growing word my child
speaks,
And sleep, my brow turned eastward,
'Til the dawn.

Türme

Am Strande nördlichen Meeres,
Wo schwarzer grausamer Sturm Schwärme gell kreischender
 Möwen peitscht,
Wo an rissige Klippen geschleuderte Woge eisgrün
 klirrend zerbricht,
Zerschellt, zerspritzt,
Starrt der Turm.
Hart, finster, lastend, stumm in grauer Öde.
Erstorben.
Ohne Mund.
Kein Tor, keine Pforte: verschlossen.
Aus blicklosen Fenstern geistert in Nebeln düsterrot
 glimmendes Licht,
Kolkt ein Rabe krächzende Prophezeiungen,
Schwimmt Schnee-Eule lautlos, flockenrieselnd in das
 kristallen singende Schweigen der Nacht. –
Irgendwo fern klagt ein Schiff im Eise . . .

Irgendwo.

Irgendwo in Böhmen senkt eine Birke schmale blond
 umflossene Wangen rötlichen Trümmern zu.
Wehmütig, mit auf der Brust gefalteten Händen.
Doch um ihren Fuß spielen Glockenblumen,
Bunter Wachtelweizen belächelt das machtlose Burgverlies,
 und Gras trauert tändelnd auf der begrabenen
 Schwelle;
Feuerfalter gaukeln in Sonne über gestürzte Mauern, über
 erloschne Geschlechter hin.

Towers

On the strand of a northern sea
Where the cruel black storm whips swarms of shrieking gulls,
Where, onto craggy cliffs, the heaving, ice-green waves break crashing,
Smashing, spraying . . .
Stands the tower.
Hard, dark, heavy, mute, in grayish desolation.
Dead.
Without a mouth.
No door, no gate: sealed off.
From sightless windows haunts in fog a dim red glimmering light,
A raven croaks his rasping prophecies,
A snowy owl swims soundless, sifting snowflakes, through the crystal singing silence of the night.—
Somewhere, far out, a ship wails in the ice . . .

Somewhere.

Somewhere amid the forests of Bohemia a birch tree bends its golden hair toward a reddish ruin.
In mourning, hands clasped at its chest.
And yet the bluebells dance around its feet,
And colored cow-wheat smiles upon the powerless dungeon tower, while grasses idle mournfully on buried walks.
Bright coppers flutter past the fallen, sunlit walls of vanished generations.

Aus gierig glänzenden Augen der blauen Haie, die spähend, schnappend in Küstengewässern sich tummeln,
Blicken die Herrn der Feste, Seelen illyrischer Seeräuber her,
Die einst den trotzig plumpen, vierschrötig niederen Bau zum Hüter blitzender Beute setzten.
O schwarze Flaggen, Kaperfahrten, waffenschlagende Plankenkämpfe mit den Venedigern!
Vorbei.
Aus den verfallenden Kammern
Läuten nicht trunken goldene Becher mehr, die blutfarbnen Weines voll sind,
Dringt auch heut nicht Fischerkindergelärm, noch der scharfe Ruch gebratenen Seefangs.
Jadeschimmernde Eidechsen huschen emsig schwänzelnd umher, tuscheln in Eidechsenmundart zusammen
Oder sitzen auf lichtumspülten, warmen Steinen geruhsam sinnend.
In dunklen Mauern gebiert das Skorpionsweibchen lebende Junge und stirbt; aber die Söhne erben der Väter Gift.

Auch dieser ist einsam,
Dem ein herrischer Mund zu sein gebot, die zeptertragende Hand eines Königs im Osten.
Doch die Krone sprang von der Stirn, und die myrrhenduftenden Prunkgewänder verdarben. —
Er aber steht und leidet.
Unsäglich leerer Himmel, der Vogelfittich und fruchtende Wolke nicht kennt, gießt brennende Bläue endlos über ihn aus;
Gluthitzen, Strahlenfluten rinnen von seinen bleichen Quadern.

Out of the greedy, gleaming eyes of steel-blue sharks that, searching, snapping, sound the coastal waters,
Stare the fortress lords, the souls of the Illyrian pirates,
Those who once had built with cumbersome, defiant walls, a squat defender of their shining loot.
Oh the black flags, Venetian prizes, and the weapon-clashing battles hull to hull!
Long gone.
In crumbling chambers now no longer sounds the drunken clang of goblets filled with blood-red wine,
Inside these walls today no shouts of fisher-children ring, no acrid smoke of roasting fish pervades.
Jade-gleaming lizards scurry, tails flicking, here and there, and whisper in their lizard languages,
Or slowly contemplate on warming, sun-washed stones.
Within dark walls the female scorpion gives birth to living young, and dies; but sons receive the poison of the fathers.

And this one too now stands alone,
Once ordered built by royal decree, commanded by an eastern emperor's sceptered hand.
But long ago the crown fell from his brow, resplendent robes, myrrh-scented, fell to dust.—
And yet the tower suffering stands.
And an enormous empty sky that harbors neither cloud nor wing pours over it an endless, burning blue.
Molten heat and floods of sunbeams run from blocks of bleached-white stone.

Die Zypresse floh. Zeder und Ölbaum sind fortgewandert,
und keine Rebe schmiegt liebende Arme um seinen schlafenden Stein.
Kein Hirt treibt die Schafe, daß sie aus erdnahen Fugen ihm staubige Gräser rupfen,
Und dem Zuge beladner Kamele zeigt er niemals den Weg.

Zuweilen,
Wenn die Sichel der Nacht des Tages glühende Garben mäht,
Ein schmaler Mond wie Balsam ihm silbrige Kühle träuft,
Bebt aus seinem Wesen
Der scheue, leise, schnell ermattete Klang
Verschollener Harfe.

Vielleicht vergaß mich meine Seele im Traum,
Sank gen Morgen gebreitet, und ihres Wandelfluges
Harrte der weiße Turm: durch seine heißen, verwunschenen, lebenlosen Gemächer irrte sie,
Ihre Ahnen suchend,
Und rührte verschwebend Saiten an, die noch tönen . . .

The cypress fled. The cedar and the olive wandered far, and
vines of grapes no longer cling to sleeping stone.
No shepherd drives the sheep to gather dusty grasses out of
low-set crevices.
And no more caravans of laden camels steer their course
toward the tower.

At times,
When night's sharp sickle reaps the glowing sheaves of day,
And a narrow moon drips silvery coolness on the tower—
There rises, vibrant, from its deepest being
The shy and gentle, quickly dying tone
Of a long forgotten harp.

Perhaps my soul forgot me in my dream,
And sank, wings spread towards morning, where the tower
stood to meet its wandering flight,
And roved through hot, enchanted, lifeless rooms,
In search of ancestors,
And touched the hovering strings that still resound . . .

Das Einhorn

Der Pfauen Pracht,
Blau, grün und gülden, blühte in Dämmerung
Tropischer Wipfelwirrnis, und graue Affen
Fletschten und zankten, hangelten, tummelten, balgten sich
im Geschlinge.
Der große Tiger, geduckt, zuckte die Kralle, starrte, verhielt,
Als das stumme seltsame Wild durch seine indischen
Wälder floh,
Westwärts zum Meere.

Das Einhorn.

Seine Hufe schlugen die Flut
Leicht, nur spielend. Wogen bäumten sich
Übermütig,
Und es lief mit der wiehernd springenden, jagenden silber-
mähnigen Herde.
Über ihnen
Schrieb Flug schwarzer Störche eilige Rätselzeichen an den
Himmel Arabiens,
Der mit sinkender Sonne eine Fruchtschale bot:
Gelbe Birnen, gerötete Äpfel,
Pfirsich, Orange und prangende Trauben,
Scheiben reifer Melone.
Schwarze Felsen glommen im Untergange,
Amethystene Burgen,
Weiße glühten, verzauberte Schlösser aus Karneol und
Topas.

The Unicorn

The peacock's radiance,
Blue, green and golden, blossomed in the shadows
Of tangled jungle treetops, and gray monkeys
Scuffled, snarled, dangled, jumped and frolicked in the vines.
The giant tiger, crouching, curled his claws and stared and waited,
As a strange and silent creature fled through Indian forests
Westward to the sea.

The unicorn.

His hooves pranced on the water
Softly, playfully. The waves reared up,
High-spirited,
And on he ran beside the snorting, hurtling, silvery-maned herd.
Above them
Black flights of storks scrawled enigmatic characters across Arabian skies,
That, with the sinking sun, became a bowl of fruit:
With yellow pears and reddish apples,
Peaches, oranges and gleaming grapes.
Ripe melon slices.
Black palisades sank smouldering,
Fortresses of amethyst,
Whites glistened as enchanted castles of carnelian and topaz.
Long lay the rosy fog above the pigeon-colored, darkening waters of the bay.

Spät hingen Rosennebel über den taubenfarb dunkelnden
Wassern der Bucht.

Das Einhorn.

Seine Hufe wirbelten Sand,
Der lautlos stäubte. Es sah
Einsame Städte, bleich, mit Kuppel und Minarett und den
Steinen der Leichenfelder
Schweigend unter dem klingenden Monde.
Es sah
Trümmer, verlassene Stätten, nur von Geistern behaust,
in funkelnder Finsternis
Unter kalten Gestirnen.
Einmal lockte der Wüstenkauz,
Und im Fernen heulten Schakale klagend;
Hyänen lachten.
Am Eingang des Zeltes unter der Dattelpalme
Hob das weiße syrische Dromedar träumend den kleinen
Kopf, und seine Glocke tönte.

Vorüber das Einhorn, vorüber.

Denn seine leichten, flüchtigen Füße kamen weither aus
dem Goldlande Ophir,
Und aus seinen Augen glitzerten Blicke der Schlangen, die
des Beschwörers Flöte aus Körben tauchen, gaukeln
und tanzen heißt,
Doch das steile Horn seiner Stirnmitte goß sanfteres Licht,
milchig schimmerndes,
Über die nackten Hände und weich umschleierten Brüste
der Frau,

The unicorn.

His hooves swirled sand
That scattered soundless. And he saw
Lone cities, pale, with domes and minarets and stones of burial grounds,
Becalmed beneath the ringing moon.
He saw
The ruins of abandoned settlements, now occupied by ghosts in sparkling darkness
Under frozen constellations.
Once the desert owl called out,
And in the distance mournful jackals howled;
Hyenas laughed.
By entrances to tents beneath the date palms
A silver Syrian dromedary lifted its small head from dreams and chimed its bell.

The unicorn ran on and on.

For his softly fleeting hooves had come from far away, out of the golden land of Ophir,
And from his eyes there gleamed the gaze of snakes that charmers' flutes dip out of baskets and command to sway and dance,
And yet the jutting horn upon his forehead shed a softer, milky shimmering light,
Across the woman's naked hands and gently veiled breasts

Die da stand
Zwischen Mannasträuchern.

Ihr Gruß:
Demut
Und der stille Glanz tiefer, wartender Augen
Und ein Hauchen, leise quellendes Murmeln des Mundes. –
Brunnen in Nacht.

As she stood waiting
By the manna bushes.

Her greeting:
Humility
And the quiet splendor of her deep, expectant eyes,
And a breath, a gentle, welling murmur of her mouth.—
A fountain in the night.

Die Tiere von Ninive

Jona, Schlußwort

Die Nacht
Neigte goldblasse Schale, und Mondmilch troff
In das kupferne Becken
Auf dem Dache des weißen Hauses,
Und eine blaugraue Katze mit Agatsteinaugen
Schlich und hockte und trank.

In einer Nische bröckelnden Tempelgemäuers
Saß Racham der Geier regungslos mit gesunkenen Flügeln
Und schlief.
Fern
Hinter den Weingärten lag an wüstem Ort ein gestürzter, verendeter Esel.
In seinem gebrochenen Blick fraßen Würmer,
Und sein Geruch ward stinkend und befleckte die reine Luft und verhöhnte den leisen Tau, der ihn netzte.
Und er harrte spitzer, fallender Fittiche, des gelben, häßlich nackten Vogelgesichts, bohrender Krallen und des zerreißenden tilgenden Schnabels,
Auf daß bestattet werde, was Erde und Wind verpestet . . .
Der Geier träumte.

Nah dem Tore der Stadt
Ruhte am Hügel, den gebogenen Stab zur Seite, ein junger Hirt.
Sein Knabenantlitz, erhoben, wie leerer empfangender Becher, füllte sich schimmernd mit dem rieselnden Licht der Gestirne,
Quoll über,

The Animals of Nineveh

Jonah, last word

The night
Tipped its pale, golden bowl, and dripping moonmilk
drained
Into the copper cup
Atop the white house,
And a blue-gray cat with agate eyes
Crept up, and crouched, and drank.

In a hollow of the crumbling temple wall
Racham the vulture sat with folded wings, unmoving.
And he slept.
Far
Behind the vineyard in a barren place lay a fallen donkey,
dead.
Into his broken eyes ate worms.
And his stench defiled the pure air and spoiled the gentle
dew that covered him.
And he awaited pointed falling wings; the ugly, naked,
yellow head; the piercing claws, and the annihilating,
tearing beak,
So what had fouled the earth and wind would soon be laid
to rest . . .
The vulture dreamed.

Close by the city gate
Upon a hill a shepherd boy lay resting by his curving staff.
His youthful face, uplifted like a waiting chalice, filled and
shimmered with the sifting light of stars,
And overflowed,

Und ihr schwebend sirrendes, singendes Kreisen in unendlichen Räumen rührte sein Ohr.
Rings zerging das weiche Vlies seiner Lämmer in dunstig dünnes Gewölk.

Ein Kind,
Kleiner, abgezehrter, schmutziger Leib,
Bedeckt mit Fetzen, bedeckt mit Schwären,
Über die Schwelle der Grabkammer hingeworfen,
Streckte sich, schlief.
Es kannte nicht Vater noch Mutter, und nur ein Hund,
Einer der Ausgestoßenen, Verachtetsten,
Gleich arm, gleich krank, geplagt und zerschrunden,
Kratzte sich, duckte den Kopf und leckte liebreich die Wange unter den strähnig schwarzen verfilzten Haaren. –
Und das Kind ballte die Faust und schlug ihn im Traum.

Und ein Sturm flog auf mit mächtigem Braus,
Ein großer Sturm fuhr von Osten auf und kam und fegte die Weide, entsetzte die Herden und wirbelte totes Geäst
Und griff wie mit Nägeln in des Propheten Bart, zerrte und zauste.

Doch Jona ging,
Und die Last über Ninive, die er geschaut, hing über seinem Scheitel.
Er aber wandelte in schwerem Sinnen. –

Von der starken Zinne des Königsschlosses schmetterte ein bemalter Stein,

While the soaring, humming song of constellations circling in unending spaces touched his ears.
And all about him soft white fleece dissolved to mist and cloud.

A child
A tiny, wasted, dirty figure
Dressed in rags and covered all with sores,
Stretched out across the entrance to a tomb,
Rolled in his sleep.
He knew no mother, knew no father, just a dog,
As poor, as sick, as tormented as he,
Stood by, and scratched himself and lowered his head to lick the cheek beneath the black and stringy, matted hair.—
And the child clenched his fist and beat him in his dream.

And a storm flew up with mighty thundering.
A great storm drove in from the East and came and swept the meadows, frightened herds, and whirled up broken limbs,
And grabbed with claws the prophet's beard and tugged and tore.

But Jonah went,
And the burden over Nineveh that he had seen, weighed on his head.
But he, in heavy brooding, strode away.—

A painted stone broke from the solid battlement atop the royal castle,

Und es heulte im Sturm und es schrie im Sturme und eine
Stimme rief:
»Um dieser willen!
Um dieser Tiere, reiner und unreiner, willen!«
Und der Gesandte des Herrn schrak und sah; aber nur
Finsternis war, und er hörte nichts als ein unablässiges
Wehen und Sausen,
Das seinen Mantel faßte und zog und schüttelte wie eines
Bittenden Hand das Kleid des unbarmherzig
Enteilenden.
Er aber kehrte sich nicht; er schritt
Und raffte und hielt den Mantel.

And there arose a howling and a shrieking in the storm, and then a voice cried out:
"For their sake!
For the sake of all the animals, clean and unclean!"
And the prophet of the Lord was frightened and looked up; but all was darkness and he heard no sound but ceaseless rush and roar
That grasped his robe and pulled and shook his garment like a pleading hand, as, merciless, he fled.
But he did not turn back; he traveled on
And close about him gathered up his robe.

Das Opfer

Ihre purpurnen Schuhe kennen den Weg, und die Spange
um ihren Knöchel weiß ihn.
So wandelt sie ohne Willen, gebunden, im Traum.
So wandeln die heißen dunkelnden Augen durch Reihen
steinerner Flügelkatzen und schwerer bemalter Säulen
zum Vorhof des Tempels,
Da ein nackter Greis in schmutzigem Lendentuche auf
winziger Pauke hämmert und endlos sein näselnder
Singsang fleht.
Die Aussätzige, von wirren Haaren verhangen, reckt
stöhnend den Arm.
Unfruchtbare seufzen Gebete.
Ein Jüngling steht hoch und steil, unbeweglich, mit breitem
bronzenen Schwert,
Und ein Wahnsinniger krümmt mit leisem verzückten
Lachen sich über rosengranitener Schwelle.
Wie sie vorüberstrebt, hascht die Kranke, Verdeckte nach
ihrem Kleide, den amarantfarbenen Säumen;
Sie aber zieht, die Wolke, an unerreichbaren Abendhimmeln
dahin.

Dreimal fragt ihre pochende Hand die kupferne Tür, die
ihr dreimal erwidert.
Ein Priester öffnet.
Sein Bart rinnt, blauer Fluß, über die linnene Bleiche des
Untergewandes, den Safran des Mantels.
Auf seiner hohen schwarzen Haube spreizt ein silberner
Vogel sich.
Er gießt Milch in rote Tonschalen, Milch der wachsweißen
Kuh mit vergoldeten Hörnern,

The Sacrifice

Her purple sandals know the way; the bracelet 'round her ankle knows it too.
And so, without a will, she wanders, bound within a dream.
And so her glowing, darkening eyes proceed past rows of stony wingéd cats and heavy painted pillars, to the outer courtyard of the temple,
Where an ancient, naked man in dirty loincloth hammers on a tiny kettledrum and wails his endless, singsong prayer.
A leper, hung with tangled hair, groans loud and stretches out his arm.
Infertile women sigh their prayers.
A young man, tall and straight, stands motionless and holds a bronze, broad-bladed sword,
A madman stoops in soft, ecstatic laughter on the rosy granite steps.
And as she passes by, the leper snatches at the amaranthine fringes of her gown;
But on she glides, a cloud in otherworldly evening skies.

Three times her knocking hand implores the copper door; three times comes the reply.
A priest admits her.
His rippling beard, dark blue, floods down across the bleached white linen of his tunic and the saffron yellow of his cloak.
Upon his high black helmet stands a silver bird with outspread wings.
He pours the milk in red clay vessels, milk of the wax-white cow with golden horns,

Trank den heiligen Schlangen,
Die ihre glatten, getuschten Leiber am Boden des düsternden
Raumes knäueln und wälzen.
Und eine größte chrysolithäugige hebt sich und lauscht und
wiegt den Bauch zu unhörbarem Liede.
Die Frau verneigt sich ihr, schirmt mit dem Finger das Auge
und küßt der Natter die Stirn. –
Sie schweigt
Und tritt hinaus in den leeren inneren Hof;
Nur perlmutterne Tauben picken Weizenkörner vom lauch-
grünen Nephrit.
Sie ängsten nicht.
Zwischen bunt beladenen Wänden hält streng und schmal
eine Ebenholzpforte sich,
Und dreimal rührt die Frau mit elfenbeinernem Stabe das
Schloß, das ihr Antwort weigert.
Sie bleibt und wartet.

Dort wird sie eingehn.
Unter dem Bilde des Abgotts mit goldenen Krötenschenkeln,
Im Rauche glimmenden Sandelholzes,
Beim Strahlen zuckenden Feuers
Wird der Fremde nahn,
Wird langsam schreiten und seine rechte Hand auf ihre Mitte
legen als ein Zeichen.
Er wird sie hinführen in den sengenden Kreis
Und ihre Brüste schauen
Und schweigend stark aus glühen Umarmungen Wollust
schmelzen.
Sie töten...
So ist es ihr vorbestimmt und sie weiß es.

The drink of sacred serpents
Who, in the fading light, lie knotted, writhing shiny, ink-striped bodies on the chamber floor.
And then the largest lifts its chrysolite-eyed head and listens, while its belly sways to melodies unheard.
The woman bows, her fingers covering her eyes, and lays a kiss upon the adder's head.—
Without a word
She steps outside into the empty inner court;
There only iridescent pigeons peck at grains of wheat upon the leek-green slabs of jade.
They cannot frighten her.
Between the color-laden walls a gate of ebony stands stern and narrow,
And there, with an ivory staff, three times the woman strikes the lock,—which gives no answer.
She stays and waits.

Here she will enter.
And beneath the image of the demigod with golden, toad-like thighs,
In the smoke of glowing sandalwood,
By the rays of the flickering fire
Will come the stranger,
Striding slowly, and will place his right hand as a sign upon her waist.
And he will lead her to within the flaming circle
And behold her breasts,
Then silently and strong will melt his lust from hot embraces.
And will kill her . . .
Thus her fate has been decided, and she knows it.

Sie zaudert nicht. Kein Beben zwingt ihre Glieder; sie blickt nicht um,
Kennt weder Glück noch Unglück.
Sie füllte sich ganz mit brennender Finsternis, mit dumpf erglänzender Demut, die dem Gebote des Scheusals dienen, dem goldenen Götzen sterben will. –

Doch in ihrem Herzen ist Gott.
Auf ihrem ernsten und schönen Antlitz haftet sein Siegel.
Das aber weiß sie nicht.

She does not hesitate. No trembling seizes her; she gazes straight ahead,
And senses neither happiness nor sorrow,
But fills herself with burning darkness and a smouldering humility—she who soon will follow the commandment of the monster, and will perish for a golden idol.—

Yet in her heart is God.
And on her grave and lovely face there burns His seal.
But this she does not know.

Der Ural

Wenn ich Finsternis packe, verwunden Schroffen
Meine Hand.
Da ist Gebirg, das mit Zacken und Schründen sich aufsteilt
und bäumt wie eines Drachen Kamm.
Da ist der Ural.
Kette von Nord nach Süd, Scheide von West und Ost, Mauer
zwischen zwei Erden.
Ich muß die Lampe löschen, daß er werde, daß er vor mir
krieche, riesiges Echsengetüm, in Nacht.
Denn es quillt sein Gestein, und sein Gewälde wächst
Aus meiner Seele.
Und der Hauch meines Mundes webt rauchig über dem
Schnee des Jaman-tau, meines ewigen Gipfels.

Ich sinne.

Plumpe, zottige Bären trollen brummend aus Höhlen,
Wolfsnasen wittern im Bruch,
Braunpelzige Zobelmarder schleichen.
Selbst schuf ich das fiedrig schreckende gelbäugige Eulen-
gesicht
Und springendem Quellfluß den großen grausilbernen Fisch
Und schwarzen Forsten schwere flügelknatternde Auerhähne,
Die immer wieder doch meines Felsenadlers goldene Kralle
schlägt und aufreißt in Lüfte ...
Aber die Wurzel großer düstermähniger Tanne stößt in
Tiefen, drängt augenlos blind unerschöpflichen Kam-
mern zu, getürmten, gehäuften Schätzen,
Die da grün sind: schlangenhäutiger Serpentin, Otter unter
den Steinen, und Malachit wie erstarrtes Laub

The Urals

When I seize the darkness, rough crags
Wound my hand.
These are the ranges, rising jagged and fissured, rearing like
a dragon's back.
These are the Urals.
Chain from North to South, boundary from West to East,
wall between two worlds.
I must put out the lamp to make it appear, to make it crawl
before me like a monster lizard in the night.
For its granite swells, its woodlands grow
Out of my soul.
And the breath of my mouth weaves like smoke over the
snow of the Yaman-tau, my eternal mountain.

I meditate.

Brute, shaggy bears shuffle grumbling out of caves,
Wolf noses sniff in the marshes,
Brown-pelted sable martens slink.
Even the feathered, frightening, yellow-eyed face of the owl
I create,
And great gray-silver fishes in bounding brooks
And in the black forests, heavy wing-rattling grouse
Which sometimes the golden talons of my eagle snatch and
rend in space . . .
But the roots of great dusky-maned pines thrust into the
depths, push—eyeless, blind—towards inexhaustible
chambers, towering piles of treasure
That are green: snake-skinned ophite, adder among
minerals, and malachite like hardened leaves,

Und hellerer Chrysopras, den Sonne nicht sehen darf, die ihm gierig den Apfelglanz aussaugt und fahlt.
Edelerz flimmert; Rubinkörner locken verstreut die Schnäbel unterirdischer hammerköpfiger Vögel.
Mandelsteine reifen, mit buntem Achat gefüllt; Chalzedon schwillt traubig;
Und brauner Marmor mit eingesprengten orangenen Muscheln
Dämmert . . .

All das ist schön.

Aber ich habe anderes noch, Widriges, Dumpfes:
Schattenschlünde, da Ungestalt hockt, Halbwesen, das mir entschlüpfte, eh ich ihm Herzschlag gab.
Stumm, erstickt schreit es nach mir, doch mich schaudert; ich blicke nicht nieder.
Es harrt der Erlösung . . .
Einmal vielleicht, einmal
In kalter, sternloser Trübe,
Wenn Windnacht leise pfeift wie ungeheure grauliche Ratte,
Baumstümpfe, faulige Stummelzähne, im Munde der Erde kaun,
Flocken gespenstisch Leichentücher erstorbenem Hochmoor breiten –
Dann werde ich hingehn
Und, meine Hände auf bebender Brust, mich dem Abgrund neigen . . .

And brighter chrysophrase which sun may never see, lest greedily it suck and pale the apple glow.
Rich ores glimmer; scattered ruby grains lure the beaks of hammerheaded subterranean birds.
Amygdaloids ripen, filled with colorful agate; chalcedony swells grapelike;
And brown marble sprinkled with orange shells
Radiates . . .

All that is beautiful.

But I have still other things, dull and hostile:
Shadowy gorges where a shapeless creature crouches, half-being that escaped before I gave it heartbeat.
Mute, smothered, it cries to me, but I shudder; I do not look down.
It waits for redemption . . .
Sometime perhaps, sometime
In cold, starless gloom
When the night wind softly whistles like a huge horrid rat,
Tree stumps, rotting broken teeth, chew in the mouth of the earth,
Snowflakes spread ghostly shrouds over lifeless upland moors—
Then I will go out
And, hands on my trembling breast, will lean over the abyss . . .

Die Mergui-Inseln

Die Mergui-Inseln sind Laich.
Hingesamt vor den Schenkel des Frosches,
Der, blaues Birma, gelbes Siam, grünes Annam,
Hockt und rudert, den Schwimmfuß Malakka in chinesische
Fluten stößt.

Nein.
Meine Mergui-Inseln baden nicht singend im indischen
Meere.
Sie tauchen aus Nachtsee schweigsam in stetig tagloses
Dämmer empor,
Kuppig, schwarzgrün bezottelt,
Widerriste ungeheurer Büffel, die in Meertiefe bräunlichen
Tang durchweiden.
Ihre Nüster kocht Schaum.
Ihre Flanke rauscht Finsternis. Fahl schwelendes Wetter-
leuchten
Zittert aus gebogenem Horn.
Verglostet . . .

Unter dornigem Struppwerk des Kamms
Ducken, mit Pferdshaaren, fluglose Vögel sich, die noch
kein Forscher erkannt hat.
Von steiniger Lichtung
Starrt mondgoldnes Auge schiefergrauer reglos gewundener
Schlange in ewigen Abend auf.
Aber in Kalksteinhöhlen,
Deren Wände zerfressen von Wellenschnauzen, zernagt sind
von Tropfenzähnen,
Feiern Meerechsen in malachitgrünem Brautschmuck
brünstige Vermählungen,

The Mergui Isles

The Mergui Isles are spawn.
Strewn out beside the long leg of a frog,
Blue Burma, yellow Siam, green Annam,
That squats and sculls and dips its foot, Malacca, into Chinese seas.

But no.
My Mergui Isles do not bathe singing in the Indian Ocean.
They rise silently from seas of night into an ever-dayless twilight,
Domed and shaggy green and black,
The withers of some giant buffaloes that graze the brownish seaweed from the ocean floor.
Their nostrils foam.
Their flanks ooze darkness. Pale sheet lightning
Smoulders flashing from their curving horns.
And dies away . . .

Under thorny bristling combs
Duck flightless, horsehair-covered birds no naturalist has yet described.
And from a stony clearing,
Out of rigid, slate-gray coils a snake's moon-golden eye stares up into eternal evening.
But in the limestone caves
Whose walls were eaten out by hungry waves and gnawed by dripping teeth,
Sea lizards dressed in malachite-green costumes celebrate their wanton weddings,

Kröpft schwarzer Geier mit kahlem, blaurotem Antlitz
scharlachflossigen Fisch,
Huschen aus Löchern dunkle Schwalben, erdbraun
beschwingt, mit veilchendüsteren Brüsten,
Blühn nelken- und safranfarb Blumentiere, atmen schon
Beute, fächeln mit Fangarmen hin,
Rollt eine große Schnecke sich in den pantherfleckigen
porzellanenen Mantel ein.
Und schlummert.

Schiffe wurden verweht.
Verweht... zerrissen... Planken treiben, Fetzen der Welt,
Die den Meißel des Werkers trägt und des Schreibenden Stift
und den Pflug und Kaufmanns Gewicht und Waage,
Tausend hastende Räder, tausend haspelnde Worte
Und das Geld. – Hier kauert im Ungestirnten
Stummes Zwielicht,
Fern sanfter Mondklage, glühenden, blitzenden Sonnen-
gesängen.
Land träumt, ummurmelt von salzig triefenden Lefzen
uralter Amme.
Dumpf weißliches Glimmen sinnt.
Nur Tier und Pflanze.
Seltsame Grottenratte, die graulich gesprenkeltes, türkis-
farbes Ei bebrütet,
Schlafstrauch, des tintige Beeren
Den Esser für eines Jahrs Hingang in Druseln lullen –
doch niemand pflückt sie geschäftig...
Stille.
Sein noch ohne Tun.

And a vulture, black, with blue-red, naked head devours a fish with scarlet fins,
Dark swallows, with their earth-brown wings and violet shaded breasts dart out of holes,
And flower-beasts with saffron and carnation colors bloom, and breathe their prey, and fan the air with tentacles;
A giant snail rolls itself into its leopard-spotted coat of porcelain.
And sleeps.

Ships are blown off course,
Away . . . and torn apart . . . Planks drift, scraps of a world that bears the workman's chisel, and the pen, the plough, the merchant's weights and scale,
A thousand rushing wheels, a thousand chattered words
And money. —Here in starless spaces cowers
Soundless twilight
Far from the softly mourning moon, or from the hot, resplendent singing of the sun.
Land dreams, surrounded by the murmuring, salt-dripping lips of the primeval mother.
A dull white brightness broods.
Animals and plants alone.
A strange cave-dwelling rat that sits upon a grayish-speckled turquoise egg,
A sleeping-bush, whose inky berries
Lull the eater into year-long slumbering—but no one picks them . . .
Silence.
Motionless existence.

Wo Schlinggerank klammernd mit mageren Armen
schuppige Zwergstämme würgt,
Unter Akaziengefieder
Bricht aus tiefgrüner Blattscheide einsame Frucht hervor,
Lang und gerundet, steil in nackter, fleischiger Röte
schwellend.
Sie wartet,
Bis Lippen leisen, schwüleren Hauches
Flüsternd durch Dickicht tasten, rühren, schauern, umhüllen:
Sie bebt,
Und die im Fruchtfleisch verborgenen Stränge gießen
zeugenden Samen aus.

Where thin-armed vines and tendrils throttle scaly stems,
Beneath the feathers of acacia leaves
A single fruit breaks from a deep green sheath of leaves,
Long and rounded, swelling steep its naked, fleshy red.
It waits,
'Til lips with feverish, gentle breath
Grope whispering through the thicket, touch, and shudder,
and envelop it:
It trembles,
And within the fruit, deep hidden veins pour forth the
fertile seed.

Asien

Mutter,
Die du mir warst, eh mich die meine wiegte,
Ich kehre heim.
Laß mich hintreten vor dich.
Laß mich still dir zu Füßen sitzen, dich anschaun, dich lernen:
Den stolzen verhüllten Wuchs, mächtig ragend von mythischem Throne,
Der da auf Säulen weißer steinerner Elefantenfüße ruht,
Zu dessen Armlehne jadezüngiger bronzener Drache wurde,
Dein ernstes sonnengelbliches Antlitz, das blauschwarzes Haar seiden umspinnt,
Die Stirn, Hegemauer großer Gedanken,
Und deine Augen, jetzt finster glänzender Obsidian,
Dann wieder samten und tief, dunkle Urwaldsblumen.
Laß an deine Gewänder mich rühren, die Ruch von Ambra und Myrrhe, von Sandel und Zimmet wehn,
Die flammenden, indischem Webstuhl entlodert,
Und jene maisblassen, drauf ein Chinesenmädchen braunen Zweig, Mandelblüte und kleine rostfarbne Falter gestickt hat.
Weise mir deine Kronen: die südliche,
Grüngoldnes Palmenlaub, perlenbetaut, von Turmalin und Smaragd, Hyazinth und Saphir durchblüht,
Und die nördliche, funkelnd von Eiskristall, mit den Aquamarintropfen der sibirischen Meere.
Meinen Scheitel streife die Hand, deren Fläche noch Duft und Schmelz persischer Früchte hält,
Und mein Ohr umspiele Schalmeiensingen, wie es David der Hirt einst in den Gefilden Beth-Lechems übte.

Asia

Mother,
Mine before my own had held me,
I am coming home.
Let me stand before you.
Let me sit in silence at your feet, and gazing up, discover you:
A proud, enshrouded figure rising mighty from your mythic throne
That rests upon the pillared feet of white stone elephants,
Its armrests jade-tongued dragons made of bronze.
I see your solemn, sun-gold face, spun round with silken blue-black hair,
Your brow, the walled preserve of noble thoughts,
Your eyes, now gleaming dark obsidian,
Now deep and somber velvet jungle flowers.
Oh let me touch your robes that breathe the scent of amber trees and myrrh, of sandalwood and cinnamon,
Your flaming robes that blazed from Indian looms,
Your robes of pale corn-yellow that a Chinese girl embroidered with a brownish twig, an almond blossom and a small, rust-colored butterfly.
Show me your crowns: the southern one,
Green-golden leaves of palm, bedewed with pearls and mixed with blooming tourmaline and emerald and hyacinth and sapphire,
And the northern one that sparkles gems of ice and aquamarine droplets from Siberian seas.
Oh brush my forehead with your hand whose palm still holds the fragrant oil of Persian fruits,
And let the singing shawm play round my ear, as David's shepherd's pipe once sang across the meadows at Beth-Lechem.

Du Sinnende, Glühende, du, die adligste, reichste und reifste der Schwestern:
Du anders als jene seltsame dunkelhäutige,
Die bald mit dem Skarabäusring ihres Fingers Einlaß fordernd an riesig steinerne Wohnungen toter Könige pocht,
Bald wieder, Straußenfeder und Muschel im wolligen Haar, Pygmäen durch Wälder treibt
Oder in Wüstenleere falbmähnige Löwen weidet.
Anders du als die kindlich jüngste, die mit des Känguruhs drolligen Sprüngen hüpft
Und Händevoll grasgrüner Sittiche über den Buschstrand des Murray ausstreut.

Anders . . .

Du hast noch die stumme unendliche Geduld,
Das Wissen vom Nicht-Tun, gewaltiger Ruhe, die in sich versunken träumt,
Dein ist die Schau,
Der rätselnde Aufblick in blaue Nacht zu leuchtend wandelnden Welten.
Du bist, ob du nicht wirkst.
Und sprichst mit dem leichten Heben schmaler gülden bestäubter Hand, mit sanfter Wendung schlangenbiegsamen Halses
Und hörst den Ruf des Saxaulhähers,
Der deiner Einöde Kysyl-kum roten Sand durchwirbelt und des Wasserquells nicht bedarf,
Und weißt das Märchen des Rock, dessen unermeßlicher Flug dein Haupt überschattet.
Um dich ist Ferne.

Oh you, great thinker, radiant one, oh you the noblest, richest, ripest of them all:
You: different from your strange and dark-skinned sister
Who, with scarab ring upon her finger, knocks to gain admittance to the giant stony dwellings of dead kings,
And then, with shells and ostrich feathers in her wooly hair, drives pygmies through the woods
Or walks with dusk-maned lions over desert wastes.
And different from your youngest sister, still a child,
Who imitates the leaping kangaroos
And scatters handfuls of green parakeets along the bush-lined Murray.

Different . . .

You still possess a silent, endless patience
And the wisdom of non-action, the enormous peace in which you lose yourself and dream;
Yours is the vision,
The mysterious gaze into the bluish night to luminous wandering worlds.
You live to be, if not to act.
And speak while lightly lifting narrow, golden-dusted hands, with gentle turnings of your serpent-supple neck,
And hear the calling of the Saxaul-Jay
That whirls the red sands up from Kysyl-kum, your wilderness, and never needs to drink from wells;
You know the legend of the Roc, whose endless flight o'ershadows your great head.
About you lies the distance.

Du sitzest,
Zaubernde hinter gläserner Wand,
Geschieden, doch nah, sichtbar, unfaßlich.
Draußen ziehn sie dahin,
Träger, die dir aus bauchigen Schiffen Ballen und Kisten
und Körbe holen, Geschenke:
Jahrmarktsglück, Flitterspiel, Klapperlärmen, billig arm-
seligen Prunk...
Draußen bettelt und nimmt und rafft dein eigenes Abbild,
Schemen,
Der Seiden, lieblich wie Krokus und Orchidee, mit häßlich
schwarzem englischen Tuch vertauschte
Und deines Sehers Sprüche, die blühenden, vieltausendjährig
verzweigten Äste, um graue Büschel dürr und
geschwätzig knisternder Blätter gab.
Sie ahmt, die gespenstische Magd, dir Herrscherin nach,
heuchelt deine Gebärde, dein Wort, stiehlt deinen
Namen,
Wenn du hinabgetaucht zum tiefen Innen unseres Sterns,
dem Bade schäumenden Feuers ...
Brenne ...
Birg voll Scham, was die Törichte blößt, deiner Mitte
Geheimnis, das Flammensamen empfing,
Und die Geborenen, Geierdämonen, laß ewiglich kreisen
über den Totentürmen,
Türmen des Schweigens ...

You sit
And work your magic from behind a wall of glass,
Departed and yet near, conspicuous and inconceivable.
Outside they move along,
The bearers who remove you from the bowels of ships in crates and bales and baskets: gifts—
A circus-charm, a tinsel trinket, noisy rattles, worthless toys . . .
Outside your imitator begs and takes and snatches, . . . a mere phantom
That can barter ugly English cloth for silks as beautiful as crocuses and orchids,
And can trade your prophets' words, the blooming branches thousands of years old, for dry gray sheaves and crackling, prattling leaves.
She mimics you, oh mistress, this gray maid, and mocks your movements and your words and steals your name,
While you have plunged down to the deepest center of our star, into the foaming bath of fire . . .
Oh burn . . .
And hide in shame all that your foolish imitator bares—your inmost secret that received the flaming seed,
And let your progeny, the vulture-demons, circle endlessly above the towers of death,
The towers of silence . . .

Translator's Note

It is not uncommon for translators of verse to present lengthy apologies for their work. Usually these attempts at justification are reactions to the translator's distress at comparing his final product with the original text. Yet the inevitable chasm that gapes between a poem and its translation cannot be bridged over with explanations or hidden behind a cloud of theoretical discussion. It can only be acknowledged—and perhaps atoned for—if the translation actually succeeds in reaching out to touch its readers.

These English versions of Gertrud Kolmar's poetry were made without recourse to a theory or methodology of translation. They attempt to be English poems as well as accurate reflections of the sound and meaning of the originals. Fortunately for me, Gertrud Kolmar is a poet of the physical world. Thus I was often spared the duty of interpreting abstract concepts (which truly comprise the "foreignness" of another language) and could point instead to the things of the world—to a realm of experience, shared by all, which exists beyond language.

My selections were based on two criteria: (1) the strength of the poems, and (2) their "translatability." Thus in a few cases I have included poems that seemed to beg for translation, but were not the most impressive originals. In other cases I was forced to omit poems that defiantly resisted the English language. And occasionally there were compromises. I sought, wherever possible, to preserve original rhyme and meter; but when a great poem faced either exclusion or rhymelessness I usually opted for the latter alternative. The reader will have slight difficulty locating these compromises, since *all* of Gertrud Kolmar's poetry (except the cycle *Welten* [*Worlds*]) is rhymed in the original.

The statement that "poems are never finished, only abandoned" is probably even more true about translations than about the original works. At any rate, I can certainly make no claim to perfection for any single line of my work. Indeed, I will vouch for the absolute "accuracy" of only one translation: the title "Sea-Monster," which Gertrud Kolmar herself applied to the poem "Meerwunder" (cf. p. 82).

My goal as a translator was a simple one: to unlock the unusual treasures of Gertrud Kolmar's work for the reader of English poetry, to remove her poems from the limbo of nonexistence so that they might enjoy a few moments of life—even if only as shadows of their original form. In this way I hope to commemorate a great soul who, thirty years ago, fell victim to the ultimate catastrophe of our times.

Notes

1. *Eine Mutter*, p. 19f.
2. Original in *Das lyrische Werk* (Munich, 1960), p. 600. Hereafter DLW.
3. DLW, 597f.
4. Letter of January 26, 1943.
5. Letter of December 15, 1940.
6. DLW, 127. Excerpts from stanzas 1 and 2.
7. DLW, 339. Cf. p. 165.
8. DLW, 371.
9. "Borzoi" from the cycle *Welten* (*Worlds*), 1937. DLW, 554.
10. Letter of November 9, 1941.
11. Letter of October 1, 1939.
12. DLW, 288.
13. Letter of February 20, 1943.
14. DLW, 556f. Cf. p. 197.
15. "Verwandlungen," DLW, 20. Cf. "Metamorphoses," p. 81.
16. *Eine Mutter*, p. 110.
17. "Fischkönig," DLW, 202.
18. *Prosa jüdischer Dichter*, p. 308. Cf. bibliography no. 10.
19. "Meerwunder," DLW, 245. Cf. p. 82.
20. DLW, 609. Note the shift of initials in her chosen pseudonym.
21. DLW, 487. Cf. p. 175.
22. DLW, 463. Cf. p. 169.
23. DLW, 531. Cf. p. 187.
24. "Mädchen," DLW, 59. Cf. "Girl," p. 67.
25. "Die Unerschlossene," DLW, 12. Cf. "Woman Undiscovered," p. 59.
26. Ibid.
27. "Die Jüdin," DLW, 36. Cf. "The Jewish Woman," p. 109.
28. DLW, 101. Cf. p. 113.

29. DLW, 102.
30. Ibid.
31. "Die Jüdin," DLW, 37.
32. DLW, 103.
33. "Verwandlungen," DLW, 20. Cf. "Metamorphoses," p. 81.
34. "Das Tier" ("The Animal"), DLW, 105f. Cited are stanzas, 4, 5 and 6.
35. "Troglodytin," DLW, 39. Cf. "Troglodyte," p. 63.
36. "Du," DLW, p. 32. Cf. "You," p. 73.
37. "Die Sünderin," DLW, 67. Cf. "The Sinner," p. 77.
38. "Mörder," DLW, 110f. Cf. p. 98.
39. "Eine Mutter," DLW, 262. Cf. "A Mother," p. 87.
40. "Komm" DLW, 222. Cf. "Come," p. 103.
41. "Wahn," ("Madness") DLW, 259f. Quoted are stanzas 1, 4 and 7.
42. Although there are astonishing similarities to a few poems by Annette von Droste-Hülshoff (1797–1848), cf. the second stanza of "Das Hirtenfeuer."
43. Gertrud Kolmar claimed not to have been influenced by Rilke, although she revered his poetry. Still there are striking similarities to Rilke in her work. Cf. "Der Panther" and "Trauerspiel" from *Tierträume.*
44. "Der Tag der großen Klage," DLW, 167f.
45. "Der Geier," DLW, 165f. (Cf. p. 136) In searching for antecedents to Gertrud Kolmar's animal poems one would do well to trace the image of the vulture. This leads us straight to the animal poems of the French "Parnassian" Charles Leconte de Lisle (1818–1894), especially "Le Sommeil du Condor."
46. Reminiscent, in part, of the fifth of Verlaine's "Ariettes Oubliées" and of Rilke's "Übung am Klavier."
47. DLW, 319. Cf. "The Fairest Wonders," p. 151.
48. First published by the Kösel-Verlag, Munich, in 1965.
49. *Eine Mutter*, 21.
50. Ibid, 23.
51. Ibid, 21.
52. Ibid, 27.
53. Ibid, 172.
54. Ibid, 235.
55. Ibid, 238.
56. Notably in "Killer Dove" (p. 145) and "Murder" (p. 99).
57. *Eine Mutter*, 230f. All ellipses are part of the original.
58. As revealed in the magazine *Sinn und Form* in March, 1972. Cf. Bibliography no. 18.
59. "Im Lager," "Anno Domini 1933," "Der Mißhandelte." Other poems in the 1933 cycle were later included in the large collection *Weibliches Bildnis* (e.g., "Wir Juden").
60. *Sinn und Form*, p. 395. The poem is dated September 17, 1933.

61. First published in *Jahrbuch der deutschen Schillergesellschaft* IX (1965).
62. Ibid, p. 579f.
63. "Paris," DLW, 381f. Quoted are stanzas 3 and 5.
64. "Die Tiere von Ninive," DLW, 580f. Cf. p. 226.
65. Letter of December 16, 1941.
66. "Aus dem Dunkel," DLW, 571f. Cf. "Out of Darkness," p. 209.
67. "Türme," DLW, 575. Cf. "Towers," p. 215. The tower symbol may have been inspired by the towers of Zion mentioned in Psalm 48.
68. "Der Ural," DLW, 585. Cf. "The Urals," p. 239.
69. "Die Mergui-Inseln," DLW, 587. Cf. p. 242.
70. "Asien," DLW, 590f. Cf. p. 248.
71. A Jewish newspaper.
72. Letter of October 16, 1938.
73. All of Gertrud Kolmar's letters had to pass official censorship. Thus they are often more revealing in what they omit than in what they disclose about the persecution of German Jews.
74. Letter of May 13, 1939.
75. Ibid.
76. Letter of October 1, 1939.
77. In which he would write from 11 P.M. until 2–3 A.M., sleep until time for work (8 A.M. to 2 P.M.), then return home and sleep again from 3 P.M. until 7:30.
78. Letter of January 15, 1940.
79. *Prosa jüdischer Dichter*, p. 298f. Cf. Bibliography no. 10.
80. Letter of August 12, 1940.
81. Letter of May 15, 1940.
82. Chaim Nachman Bialik (1873–1934), Russian-born poet, creator of some of the greatest Hebrew and Yiddish verse.
83. Letter of July 14, 1940.
84. Letter of July 19, 1942.
85. Letter of October 23, 1941.
86. Letter of December 15, 1942.
87. Letter of January 13, 1943.
88. Apparently her last work, this story, like the Hebrew poems, has been lost.
89. Letter of July 19, 1942.
90. Letter of December 15, 1942.

Bibliography

The following bibliography includes all known publications of works by Gertrud Kolmar, with the exception of individual poems appearing in German anthologies after 1945.

1. *Gedichte*. Berlin: Egon Fleischel & Co., 1917.
2. "Die Gauklerin," "Die Entführte." *Insel Almanach auf das Jahr, 1930*. Leipzig: Insel Verlag, 1930, pp. 93–96.
3. "Die Fahrende, Das Räubermädchen, Die Ottern, Die Sinnende." *Herz zum Hafen. Frauengedichte der Gegenwart*, eds. Elisabeth Langgässer and Ina Seidel. Leipzig: R. Voigtländers Verlag, 1933, pp. 125–128.
4. "Ein Mädchen" (= DLW: "Ein anderes"), "Ein grünes Kleid." *Der weisse Rabe* II 1/2 (February, 1933) pp. 15–16.
5. "Wappen von Allenburg." *Der weisse Rabe* II 5/6 (June/July, 1933) p. 39.
6. "Wappen von Liebemuhl, Wappen von Ahlen." *Der weisse Rabe* III 1/2 (March, 1934) pp. 33–34.
7. *Preussische Wappen*. Berlin: Verlag Die Rabenpresse, 1934.
8. *Die Frau und die Tiere. Gedichte*. Berlin: Jüdischer Buchverlag Erwin Löwe, 1938. (Published under the name Gertrud Chodziesner.)
9. *Welten*. Berlin: Suhrkamp Verlag, 1947.
10. "Verwandlungen, Die Drude, Leda, Hafenstadt, Meerwunder, Das Tier, Wir Juden, Die Kinderdiebin, Hexe, Der Tag der Großen Klage, Dem Feinde, Hyänen, Beerensammlerinnen, Der Schwimmer, Der Sohn, Abschied." *Sinn und Form*, I 2 (1949), pp. 11–27.
11. "Abschied," "Wir Juden"/"Parting," "We Jews." *Commentary* X, November, 1950. Reprinted in *Jewish Frontier*, March, 1960.
12. *Das lyrische Werk*. Heidelberg/Darmstadt: Verlag Lambert Schneider, 1955.
13. "Susanna." *Das leere Haus. Prosa jüdischer Dichter*, ed. Karl Otten. Stuttgart: Cotta Verlag, 1959, pp. 293–336.

14. *Das lyrische Werk.* München: Kösel Verlag, 1960.
15. "Das Einhorn/The Unicorn," "Die alte Frau/The Old Woman." *Modern German Poetry 1910–1960*, eds. Michael Hamburger and Christopher Middleton. New York: Grove Press, 1962 (also: London: MacGibbon & Kee, Ltd., 1962).
16. *Tag und Tierträume.* München: Deutscher Taschenbuch Verlag, 1963.
17. *Eine Mutter.* München: Kösel Verlag, 1965.
18. "Das Bildnis Robespierres," ed. Johanna Zeitler. *Jahrbuch der deutschen Schillergesellschaft* IX (1965), pp. 553–580.
19. *Die Kerze von Arras. Gedichte.* Berlin: Aufbau Verlag, 1968.
20. *Briefe an die Schwester Hilde (1938–1943)*, ed. Johanna Zeitler. München: Kösel Verlag, 1970.
21. "Im Lager," "Anno Domini 1933," "Der Mißhandelte." *Sinn und Form* XXIV 2 (March, 1972), pp. 395–398.